WHAT PEOP
ABOUT *SPEED OF UNITY*...

BRIAN HOUSTON

Global Senior Pastor, Hillsong Church

Rob is a gifted communicator who has the unique ability to lift your perspective to dream bigger, believe for more, and look to the future with reenergized passion and zeal. Unity is not a man-made concept, but a God-breathed reality; for where there is unity, God's blessing also resides. I believe the principles and lessons recorded within these pages will help unlock greater purpose within you—as my friend Rob says, "Nothing is impossible when you're moving at the speed of unity."

LISA BEVERE

New York Times Bestselling Author, Co-founder, Messenger International

There couldn't be a more relevant topic for leaders right now than how to foster unity. In a world that seems more separated and divided than I have ever seen, being given the tools to bring about unity and togetherness is a priceless gift.

MILES MCPHERSON

Founder of Rock Church San Diego, Author of *The Third Option*

There couldn't be a more relevant topic for leaders right now than how to foster unity. In a world that seems more separated and divided as I have ever seen, being given the tools to bring about unity and togetherness is a priceless gift.

CHRIS HODGES

Senior Pastor, Church of the Highlands, Author of *The Daniel Dilemma* and *Out of the Cave*

Rob Ketterling knows that today's leaders, perhaps more than ever, need biblical wisdom and practical solutions for uniting their teams and communities—and in *Speed of Unity,* he provides them in abundance. Drawing on his own balanced approach and lessons learned, Rob shares timeless principles of unity and vision for anyone who wants to make an eternal difference.

SAM CHAND

Leadership Consultant and author of *Harnessing the Power of Tension*

I've known Pastor Rob Ketterling up close and personal. I have read his books. I have heard him speak on major platforms. I have observed his leadership with great interest. However, his latest book, *Speed of Unity,* epitomizes who he is at his core. This book will take you on a journey of hope, and it will help you in the most pragmatic ways. As you read it, you will realize he's speaking for you and to you, challenging you to personify the *Speed of Unity*. This is an exceptionally relevant resource for any leader to utilize in staff meetings, small groups and other leadership forums.

DOUG CLAY

General Superintendent, Assemblies of God

Rob Ketterling has done it again. He has brought forward an excellent book to address a relevant topic . . . unity. Drawing from his own experiences, Rob gives leaders a great resource to foster unity with their teams.

HERBERT COOPER

Senior Pastor of People's Church

There aren't many leaders who think like Rob. His relatable stories and practical lessons push people to become better leaders and have better teams. This book's message of unity is spot-on for leaders in today's divided world!

CRAIG GROESCHEL

Pastor of Life Church and New York Times Best Selling Author

Rob Ketterling has a gift of telling stories, but his stories aren't just to entertain us. In *Speed of Unity*, he illustrates the principles of unity and vision with humor and wisdom so we can lead more effectively, build stronger teams, and help others pursue unity like never before.

NONA JONES

Facebook Head of Faith Partnerships and Author

Many leaders are looking for the latest, greatest strategic tips to build their organizations and extend their reach, but Rob Ketterling expertly illustrates that we need unity more than strategies. Unity of heart, mind, purpose and vision are the key ingredients to produce lasting results. This book is necessary for anyone given the privilege of influencing others and directing their energy toward a shared goal.

SPEED OF UNITY

FOREWORD BY JOHN MAXWELL

SPEED OF UNITY

YOU'LL KNOW IT WHEN YOU FEEL IT

ROB KETTERLING

Author's note: The anecdotes throughout this book are all true, although some names have been changed to ensure anonymity for the person(s) involved.

ISBN: 978-0-9863320-6-7

Cover design by Annie Judd

Interior formatting by Anne McLaughlin, Blue Lake Design.

Published by River Valley Publishing

Printed in the United States

CONTENTS

Foreword 11

Preface 13

Chapter 1 **The Secret Ingredient** 21

Chapter 2 **First Gear: The Speed of Agreement** 39

Chapter 3 **Second Gear: The Speed of Vision** 53

Chapter 4 **Top Gear: The Speed of Unity** 67

Chapter 5 **Make It Happen!** 85

Chapter 6 **Get People on Board** 101

Chapter 7 **Big Tower, Wrong Goals** 123

Chapter 8 **You'll Know It When You Feel It** 137

Chapter 9 **Protect Unity** 149

Chapter 10 **Unstoppable** 165

Endnotes 175

Acknowledgments 179

About the Author 181

River Valley Network 183

Resources 185

FOREWORD

For a while now, I've experienced something I'm calling, "leadership sadness." As I look around the world, I see a stunning lack of leadership at all levels of culture. And I know it's a lack of leadership because when I look at different communities and countries—including America—I see a lack of *unity*.

It's not only present in politics, however. I've seen organizations with exceptional missions that are full of division and disunity. I've seen families that can't spend holidays together because they can't agree on one issue. I've met men and women who cannot set aside their agenda for even one second in order to connect with others. And it's costing us more than we could ever imagine.

That's why I'm "leadership sad"; because, as a leader, you must lead people from all walks, backgrounds, and perspectives. People who can't learn to move forward despite their disagreements will inevitably crash. As Abe Lincoln famously said, borrowing from the Bible, "A house divided against itself cannot stand."

Division is a roadblock to both success and significance. Unity is what moves us forward towards a better future.

I have known Rob for over a decade, and our friendship is such a gift. He is a world-class leader, author, and pastor, and he fights for unity with tremendous passion which I've heard countless times. Whether he's on the golf course or on the stage, Rob's heart overflows with stories of betrayal and pain that turned into redemption and forgiveness. I've seen the *Speed of Unity* modeled in his beautiful family and his incredible church and I know you will see that same breakthrough through as a result of this book.

If I can share one more thing with you, I want to remind you that *unity* does not mean *uniformity*; diverse teams are strong teams, and while they *will* disagree at time, if they are unified they can move forward together. I'd also remind you that speed doesn't mean shortcuts; challenges will come, and you will have to fight to stay focused on what truly matters. You've found the right tool in *Speed of Unity* to guide you and the teams you lead into a brighter future.

I know Rob's lessons will provoke your thinking, and you will want to make the neccessary changes to see the *Speed of Unity* in action. But I don't know of a better person than Rob to learn from on this topic. My friend, there is an untapped speed in you, and I'm excited for you to find it! Follow Rob's lead and find the *Speed of Unity*!

Dr. John C. Maxwell
#1 *New York Times* bestselling author and leadership expert

PREFACE

Everything changed on the way to finishing this book. I wrote the manuscript in the early months of 2020, but the final edits took a backseat to a few things that increasingly occupied my attention: a global pandemic, economic distress, skyrocketing unemployment, racial unrest, rioting and looting, conflict over statues, defiance about masks, divisive political language, and, oh yeah, Becca and I got COVID-19. Other than that, things have been pretty normal for us.

George Floyd tragically died just a few miles from where I'm writing these words. In days, Minneapolis became the epicenter of chaos in our country. This book is about the amazing power of unity to bring good to every corner of a society, but in the past few months, we've been hurtling in the opposite direction. On virtually every topic, we've spiraled downward into fierce positions of "us versus them."

We've always had disagreements, but this is different. The level of suspicion of other people's motives (and their sanity) is far higher than before, and insisting on our "rights" makes people feel completely justified in their fury. Jesus warned, "Any kingdom divided by civil war is doomed. A town or family splintered by feuding will fall apart" (Matthew 12:25). More than a century and a half ago, Abraham Lincoln echoed these words of Jesus in one of his most famous speeches. At the time, in 1858, our nation was being torn apart by the issue of slavery. Lincoln told the Republican Party delegates in Springfield, Illinois, "A house divided against itself cannot stand. . . . I do not expect the Union to be dissolved—I do not expect the house to fall—but I do expect that it will cease to be divided."[1] It ceased to be divided, but it took hundreds of thousands of lives to bring the country together again, and even then, bitterness lingered for generations.

A crisis doesn't create character as much as it reveals it. We desperately need unity of heart and action to address the pandemic and the accompanying economic downturn, but everywhere we turn, we see sniping and division. In the face of the spread of the virus and the mounting death toll, we need a unified front of scientists and political leaders who will come together to chart the best course forward. Is that too much to ask?

Unity is a powerful ray of light in the darkest times. After the tragic death of George Floyd and the riots that followed, the reactions in our community were literally night and day. During the morning hours, people from our church and churches all over the city showed up on the streets to sweep and shovel broken glass, stack bricks where walls had been torn down the night before, and help store owners board up their shops. We took food to families in the devastated neighborhoods and provided meals for the police and National Guard troops. We partnered with many other churches and organizations to care for the people of our city. We didn't choose sides; we're for everybody. So many people came to care for the neighborhood that by 10:00 each morning, all the damage from the night before had been cleaned up. The people who showed up each morning demonstrated a heartfelt love for people, and love propelled our unity of action.

But the nights were a different story. Peaceful demonstrations provided cover for extremists. Vandalism, rioting, looting, random violence, and Molotov cocktails shattered the peace and created terror among residents of the city. All the good that had happened during the day was destroyed in the darkness and firelight. I received frantic calls every night from people in our church who wanted to know what to do, and every night I sat in our living room watching the news with a shotgun on the ottoman in front of me. Were my fears overblown? Maybe, but people who ask that question weren't here. They didn't see what we saw and hear what we heard.

In the middle of all this, Becca went to a graduation event. A few days later, she started running a fever and felt fatigued. Her parents were coming for a visit, so I suggested she get tested for COVID. It was positive, so she had to quarantine for fourteen days. The doctor told her that since I didn't have any symptoms, she might want to quarantine from me during that time. However, I was pretty sure I'd get it since we'd been together, and indeed, I did. Both of us had fevers, body aches, and exhaustion. We slept hard every night, got up, then took naps after a couple of hours, got up again, and took naps again throughout the day. We lost our sense of taste and smell. As a side benefit, we used this occasion to eat everything in our pantry we didn't want to eat. Many people had recommended this food or that one, but when we tried them, they tasted terrible! Now we could eat them without retching.

Last year, a visitor from Africa told me, "One of the most beautiful things about America is its predictability. It allows people to plan for the future and create forward momentum. Predictability is the fertile soil where prosperity can grow." It's a brilliant observation, but in the past several months, American predictability has taken a big hit. Millions are out of work, the government sometimes can't decide how to help, we hear competing messages about how to flatten the curve of the virus, and calls for racial justice demand that people take sides. Fights have broken out because someone wasn't wearing a mask. Homeowners have stood in front of their homes with assault rifles as angry demonstrators marched by. Some of the protesters are moms who are trying to protect their children, but others are armed and armored like they're in special ops. The mood on the streets feels a lot like The Hunger Games.

The fracturing of unity isn't only "out there." As the states began reopening in April and May, churches had to decide whether to go back to in-person worship services. Suddenly, I could relate to Dr. Anthony Fauci, our nation's chief epidemiologist who catches flak from all sides. People in our church had (and still have) passionate perspectives: Some insist the virus isn't that bad, and it's crazy for the country to destroy itself economically with shutdowns. These people can't understand why we ever closed the church in the first place, and they think closing means fear wins. A second group advocates opening the church for worship under workable guidelines of masks and social distancing. A third set of people believe any risk isn't worth taking, so they don't want to open until a vaccine has reduced the virus to almost no cases. They wonder if I've lost my mind to even consider reopening while there are still infections in our community. In fact, one email accused me of trying to kill people with the virus!

These three major opinions have different assumptions, but they share one thing in common: they're all convinced that those who disagree with them aren't just wrong, they're evil. I've heard some of the most hateful language from people who hold one of these views (or a variation), and fiercely condemn anyone who has a different opinion. Some people who had been friends for years disagree about reopening the church and now consider each other to be enemies. I never thought I'd see anything like this.

Where do we go from here? How do we find unity among the chaos? The rest of this book is designed for a broad audience—people in the church as well as those in business, medicine, agriculture, the arts, and every other field—but I want to put on my pastor's hat and be unreservedly spiritual. (If you're not interested in my views of the biblical and spiritual solutions, you can skip the rest of the Introduction.) This is what I believe: Our only hope to bridge the divisions in our country today is the love of Jesus Christ. In the apostle Paul's sweeping letter to the Romans, he doesn't mince words when he describes our condition apart from Christ. We had nothing to impress God, no way to twist His arm to get Him to accept us. We were "utterly helpless." "But God showed his great love for us by sending Christ to die for us while we were still sinners. . . . our friendship with God was restored by the death of his Son while we were still his enemies" (Romans 5:6, 8, 10). If we can't love those who disagree with us, it shows that we haven't yet grasped the wonder that God loved us when we didn't just disagree with Him—we were His utterly helpless enemies!

In the ancient world in the time of Jesus, ethnic hatred was a permanent fixture in the lives of the Jews. They despised half-breed Samaritans and the Gentiles, a designation which included everyone on the planet who wasn't Jewish. The gospel of grace doesn't just change individuals; it radically transforms our relationships with people who aren't like us.

The temple in Jerusalem was divided by a wall that separated Jews from believing Gentiles. The wall was a symbol of segregation, of "better than," of "not really one of us." But Paul explains that the grace of God destroys the wall between us: "For Christ himself has brought peace to us. He united Jews and Gentiles into one people when, in his own body on the cross, he broke down the wall of hostility that separated us. . . . He made peace between Jews and Gentiles by creating in himself one new people from the two groups. Together as one body, Christ reconciled both groups to God by means of his death on the cross, and our hostility toward each other was put to death" (Ephesians 2:14-16). When we talk about "those people," we show that we really don't yet understand the depth of God's love for all people. In the warmth of His love, hostility itself is put to death!

Today, we're quick to identify our differences: Republican or Democrat, ultra-right or progressive, mask proponent or anti-masker, tear down the statues or honor our heritage, in-person or online worshiper, and on and on. When we exclude "them" from the community of humanity—people of inestimable value because they're created in the image of God—we're forgetting that the love of Jesus changes everything. Paul tells us, "There is no longer Jew or Gentile, slave or free, male and female. For you are all one in Christ Jesus" (Galatians 3:28).

WHEN WE EXCLUDE "THEM" FROM THE COMMUNITY OF HUMANITY—PEOPLE OF INESTIMABLE VALUE BECAUSE THEY'RE CREATED IN THE IMAGE OF GOD—WE'RE FORGETTING THAT THE LOVE OF JESUS CHANGES EVERYTHING.

The apostle John wrote a lot about the necessity and the power of love. It's not enough just to use the word; we need to show the same kind of love Jesus did when He patiently and persistently reached out to everyone—the believers and unbelievers, the grateful and the defiant. John gives us God's expectation of all who call themselves Christians: "Dear children, let's not merely say that we love each other; let us show the truth by our actions. Our actions will show that we belong to the truth, so we will be confident when we stand before God" (1 John 3:18-19).

Some might insist, "Yeah, but times are tougher now than back then." Oh, really? Jesus, Paul, and John lived during a time of political polarization in the Roman occupation, severe ethnic and racial divisions, and economic privation for many. Sound familiar? Yes, I thought so. Christians should be—and can be—the leading edge in creating a culture of love and unity. When we live as lights in a dark world, when we choose to love our enemies instead of despising them, and when we sacrifice for the sake of those who are on the other side, God will use us as a catalyst for real change in our country.

Is that even possible? I believe it is. In the first three centuries after Christ, Christians gave their lives for their unbelieving neighbors during two devastating plagues. These Christians were humble enough to love people who didn't love them, and they were strong enough to sacrifice themselves for the good of people outside the faith. They changed the world through their love for others. At the beginning of this time, there were only a handful of Christians; by the end, half of the Roman Empire believed in Christ.

In the stress and anger of this moment (and every other moment, for that matter), we need a life-transforming, soul-shaping experience of God's amazing love. It's more than saying we're Christians, it's more than going to church, and it's more than reading the Bible and praying. Those activities can deepen our connection to God, or they can inoculate us from the real thing. When the love of God has penetrated our hearts, we're secure enough that we're not threatened by uncertainty and disagreements. We trust that we're in the hands of a good and great Savior who always knows what's best for our good and His glory. We have wisdom and peace in the midst of chaos. And because we're convinced that Jesus paid the ultimate price to love us when we were so unlovable, we can genuinely love those who are very different from us.

After the all-consuming distractions of the last few months, it's time to finish this manuscript. But I couldn't finish it without a new beginning—of the book and of a push for unity in our culture. I feel the need to preach a little in the preface. The rest of the book doesn't have this tone, but pointing us back to the love of Jesus is essential.

Love is the starting point, the power source, and the staying power of genuine unity.

LOVE IS THE STARTING POINT, THE POWER SOURCE, AND THE STAYING POWER OF GENUINE UNITY.

CHAPTER 1

THE SECRET INGREDIENT

Good teams become great ones when the members trust each other enough to surrender the Me for the We.

PHIL JACKSON

When I travel around the country and the world to speak at events, people often come up to me and ask, "What's the secret of your success?" I know what they're really saying. They're too polite to put it this way, but what they mean is this: "There are about 380,000 churches in the United States. River Valley Church has become one of the fifty largest, your staff members stay so long because they love it there, and you gave away more than $5 million last year to worthy causes . . . but Rob, you're just not that sharp! Do you have some kind of magic formula? You're obviously getting a greater return on your effort than I am, and I just don't get it."

I want to say, "Hey, I really *am* that sharp!" but it would be a lie. There's a very good answer to this spoken or unspoken question, one that applies to every type of organization.

When I talk to successful business leaders, I ask a similar question: "How did you rise to the top? What's your secret?" These entrepreneurs have created terrific products or innovative services, they've captured significant market share, and their revenues have gone through the roof, but some of them have responded, “I . . . I’m not sure. I guess I’ve been lucky.”

I want to yell at them, “It can’t be luck! There has to be more than that!” But I just say, “Let me dig a little deeper.” As I talk with them in more depth—and especially when I spend time with their people—I can sense that the atmosphere of each company has a powerful if intangible interpersonal synergy. Their companies are tremendously successful because the efforts of the individuals produce results that are far greater than the sum of the parts. They stimulate each other’s creativity, passion, and commitment. They’re talented friends with a common, compelling purpose, and the results are phenomenal.

That’s the same reason our church has grown so much so fast—the business leaders’ employees and our staff and volunteers have found the secret: we’re working at *the speed of unity*.

By the way, you probably noticed the image on the cover of this book. From the time I was a boy, I’ve been fascinated by the incredible precision and amazing acrobatics of the Navy Blue Angels and the Air Force Thunderbirds. They fly at 500 miles an hour, doing intricate loops, with only 36 inches from wingtip to wingtip! These pilots are the perfect example of a team operating at the speed of unity. John Foley, a former pilot with the Blue Angels described the pilots’ complete commitment to teamwork:

> “Glad to Be Here” was a statement of belief that we shared on the Blue Angels team. It was our centerpoint, our purpose larger than self. Reflecting back on my experiences, it’s clear to me that those four words were really the “secret sauce” of our high-performance team. Sometimes “Glad to Be Here” meant that we were thankful for the opportunity to be a Blue Angel.

> Sometimes it meant that we were thankful for being surrounded by a great team of high-performing individuals. And sometimes it meant that we were just grateful for being alive.
>
> Always, however, "Glad to Be Here" was our mind-set. It expressed our joy, our awareness, and our readiness to perform at the highest levels. It was a statement of our love, our commitment, our trust, and our respect for everyone on the Blue Angels team, pilots and support crew alike. Each time a member of the Blue Angels said, "Glad to Be Here," the special bond was reaffirmed and strengthened.[2]

Isn't that the kind of team you want to build and lead? Isn't that the kind of team you want to be part of? That's what this book is all about.

BEYOND THE SUPERSTAR

Many leaders assume that if they can sharpen their skills to become a superstar, they'll attract faithful and dedicated people to help them fulfill their goals. There's certainly nothing wrong with honing our talents, but the kind of success I'm talking about doesn't depend on one person.

In his #1 bestselling book, *Good to Great,* researcher Jim Collins and his team studied the factors that separated good companies from great ones. He and his team carefully analyzed the performance of 1,435 companies over forty years. They discovered what made eleven of them truly outstanding, and they identified the factors that kept the others from becoming great. Collins found that one of the most common limiting factors is reliance on one person's brilliance. In an interview about the book with *Fast Company,* he commented, "There is a direct relationship between the absence of celebrity and the presence of good-to-great results. Why? First, when you have a celebrity, the company turns into 'the one genius with 1,000 helpers.' It creates a sense that the whole thing is really about the CEO. At a deeper level, we found that for leaders to make something great, their ambition has to be for the greatness of the work and the company, rather than for themselves."[3]

The sports world has always featured the superstar players: Pele, Messi, Ronaldo, and Neymar in soccer; Jim Brown, Johnny Unitas, and Tom Brady in football; Michael Jordan, Magic Johnson, and LeBron James in basketball; and Babe Ruth, Kirby Puckett, and Mariano Rivera in baseball. (I'm sure I left out the favorites of a lot of people, but please, don't text me your complaints!) But it takes more than one superstar to win championships.

Legendary basketball coach Phil Jackson chronicled his coaching philosophy in his book, *Eleven Rings: The Soul of Success.* Professional basketball is studded with studs—in my opinion, the finest physical specimens with the most athletic talent of any athletes in the world. As the coach of the Chicago Bulls, who had Michael Jordon and Scottie Pippen on the team, and as the coach of the Los Angeles Lakers with Shaquille O'Neal, Magic Johnson, and Kobe Bryant, Jackson understood that the secret to winning championships wasn't to rely on individual greatness—it was to create greatness as a team. He writes, "Basketball is a great mystery. You can do everything right. You can have the perfect mix of talent and the best system of offense in the game. You can devise a foolproof defensive strategy and prepare your players for every possible eventuality. But if the players don't have a sense of oneness as a group, your efforts won't pay off. And the bond that unites a team can be so fragile, so elusive."[4]

Jim Collins and Phil Jackson have discovered the secret of unparalleled success: unity. It can happen anywhere, in any organization, no matter the size. When I walk into a Chick-fil-A restaurant, I sense the atmosphere is different from other places I might grab a bite. Even though it's an extensive chain of franchises, the company's leaders have infused their corporate culture with optimism, kindness, and a commitment by every employee to make every customer's experience special.

JIM COLLINS AND PHIL JACKSON HAVE DISCOVERED THE SECRET OF UNPARALLELED SUCCESS: UNITY. IT CAN HAPPEN ANYWHERE, IN ANY ORGANIZATION, NO MATTER THE SIZE.

In the hotel industry, Ritz-Carlton has a reputation for stellar customer service, not just by the people at the concierge desk, but by every employee in every role. Their internal message is: "We are ladies and gentlemen serving ladies and gentlemen." One of their corporate policies is to authorize their 40,000 employees to spend up to $2000 to satisfy the desire of any guest. The policy applies to the people who work in housekeeping up through the company organizational chart to the CEO, in all of their ninety-seven hotels in thirty countries and territories. In a *Forbes* interview, the company's former president and CEO, Simon Cooper, explained:

> The concept is to do something, to create an absolutely wonderful stay for a guest. Significantly, there is no assumption that it's because there is a problem. It could be that someone finds out it's a guest's birthday, and the next thing you know

> there's champagne and cake in the room. A lot of the stuff that crosses my desk is not that they overcame a problem but that they used their $2,000 to create an outstanding experience. There are stories about hiring a carpenter to build a shoe tree for a guest; a laundry manager who couldn't get the stain out of a dress after trying twice flying up from Puerto Rico to New York to return the dress personally; or when in Dubai a waiter overheard a gentleman musing with his wife, who was in a wheelchair, that it was a shame he couldn't get her down to the beach. The waiter told maintenance, who passed word, and the next afternoon there was a wooden walkway down the beach to a tent that was set up for them to have dinner in. That's not out of the ordinary, and the general manager didn't know about it until it was built.[5]

The employees at Ritz-Carlton don't work according to rigid rules that stifle their creativity and enthusiasm; instead, they're empowered to use company resources to do anything and everything to fulfill their purpose of giving each guest a memorable—no, a *spectacular*—stay. Together, from top to bottom, they've created a truly great company.

You don't have to have a huge international organization to create a powerful environment of unity and commitment. R. C. Colvin is a friend of mine who ran a very successful Buckle clothing store. When people walked through the doors of his store, they immediately sensed his joy and delight in serving them. I've seen the impact on everybody in the store. Employees have breathed the air of the culture R. C. has created, and they've become like him, and the faces of shoppers brightened as they felt the genuine love emanating from R. C. and his team. (He told me about the unofficial "Buckle challenge." He asks his staff: "Is it possible for someone to walk into his store and out without being greeted by one of the employees?" From what I've seen, the answer is "no!") My son Logan worked at Buckle and was trained by R. C. to truly enjoy serving customers. But Logan didn't just learn to be nice to people; R. C. pushed him to *be* better and *do* better, and in the supportive environment, Logan thrived. Later, he went to work for Nordstrom, and he implemented the lessons R. C. ingrained in him in his new environment. Within six months he became the top salesperson at the Mall of America. It's safe to say that R. C.'s incredibly positive impact on Logan will last for the rest of my son's life.

UNITY IS CONTAGIOUS, AND IT'S TRANSFERABLE.

Unity is contagious, and it's transferable. Logan became a carrier of the joy and excellence he absorbed in R. C.'s presence. To change metaphors, unity is a positive tsunami on any team in any organization. It simply can't be stopped!

THREE GEARS

Over the years, I've observed organizations moving at three distinctly different speeds:

First gear: Some operate at *the speed of agreement*.

The management and the employees have a transactional relationship, "work for pay," with very little passion or creativity to accomplish something bigger than themselves. People often see others as impediments to their performance or as competition for advancement—in other words, a threat to their transaction with the company or church.

Second gear: Others are moving at *the speed of vision*.

These organizations move much faster than the speed of agreement. The leadership team has a clear, compelling sense of purpose, and they marshal their resources to make it happen. "Vision" has been the buzzword for churches and businesses over the past couple of decades. Identifying a clear, preferred future and charting a path to get there enlist the excellence of everyone involved. Most of us have assumed that the speed of vision is as fast as we can go. It's not.

Top gear: A few organizations have learned to move at *the speed of unity*.

This gear has the intangible quality present in Chick-fil-A restaurants, Ritz-Carlton hotels and resorts, and R. C.'s Buckle store. The *motive* of those involved isn't limited to personal achievement; they're more interested in winning as a team. Their *means* is the power of synergy as they encourage each other to achieve what they could never do on their own. The *mark* of these organizations is their obvious joy in working together. And the *measure* of their effectiveness is evident in the exponential results they accomplish. This is the story of the good-to-great companies in Jim Collins's research, and it's the story of Phil Jackson's leadership in Chicago and Los Angeles with great players who didn't always play well together and win championships before he arrived. It has become the story of River Valley Church, and it can be the story of your organization, too.

REVERSE

From my observation, a lot of organizations are moving very slowly at the speed of agreement . . . but sometimes they can't even agree on the most basic transactions, like showing up on time and doing acceptable work. The people involved often are preoccupied with their personal problems and priorities, so they don't give their best to their tasks. Their goal is to get a paycheck, so they tolerate the boss and each other so they can put in their time. Other organizations and teams live with unresolved (and usually unaddressed) tension. The constant stress erodes trust and causes people to think more about defending themselves and protecting their turf than working together to accomplish great things. And some organizations live with a toxic brew of resentment, fear, misunderstanding, and bitterness. Communication takes the form of gossip, blaming, and ridicule. I ought to know. I've been there.

Years ago, I was on the staff of a church, and to put it mildly, we didn't like each other. We weren't even moving at the speed of agreement—we were at the speed of resentment, which is reverse! Each of us became very territorial. We put labels with our names on them on just about everything to be sure we didn't have to share any resources, like reams of paper, tape, staplers, and virtually everything else. Our unstated but very obvious motto was: "It's only about *me,* not about *we.*" All of us jockeyed for resources, attention, and power, and we used every means to get them, especially tearing others down so we would look smarter and more accomplished by comparison.

Competition can be wonderfully stimulating and positive, but this kind was incredibly toxic. I spent much of every day trying to figure out how to isolate my results and have more clout than the others on the team. We hardly spoke to each other in the office. We shut our doors and avoided each other as much as possible. And of course, we didn't spend any time together outside our duties. If staff lunch on Mondays hadn't been free, I'm not sure any of us would have gone. Many of the people on the team were high performers, but we really couldn't stand each other. (And this was a church staff team supposedly proclaiming the love of Jesus!)

One afternoon the music leader glared at me and sneered, "Hey, Rob, I noticed that you took hour and a half for lunch. That's a little long, isn't it?"

This wasn't a casual comment, and he wasn't trying to be helpful. It was another of his digs. I was incensed: "I was meeting with someone who needed my help." I paused for a second and then let it fly: "Don't *ever* think you need to keep track of how I spend my time! If you do this again, you and I will have issues!"

Our senior pastor wanted us to get along, but he felt powerless to create an environment with even basic civility. During my tenure on this team, I spent a lot of time processing my experiences in a journal. When another staff member accused me, in front of the senior pastor, of being irresponsible, I said, "Wait right here." I went to my office and got my journal. When I came back, I read entries documenting times when the staff member had failed to do his job, complete with dates and details. It was him, not me, who had been irresponsible. I had proof, and I was thrilled to pin the blame on him. My journal was my saving grace to avoid unwarranted blame, but this moment did nothing to promote understanding and trust. Not long afterward, virtually every person on the team left because none of us could stand it any longer.

THE COST OF DISUNITY

The cost of disunity is wide and high—it affects every aspect of our lives. Extensive research on the multiple impacts of stress show that destructive relational tension affects us physically, emotionally, socially, and spiritually.[6] One of the things I've noticed is that disunity crushes creativity. An article in *Harvard Health Publishing* cites research by Dr. Kerry Ressler, chief scientific officer at McLean Hospital and professor of psychiatry at Harvard Medical School:

> Researchers believe that when one part of your brain is engaged, the other parts of your brain may not have as much energy to handle their own vital tasks, he says. For example, if you are in a dangerous or emotionally taxing situation, the amygdala (the part of your brain that governs your survival instincts) may take over, leaving the parts of your brain that help to store memories and perform higher-order tasks with less energy and ability to get their own jobs done. "The basic idea is that the brain is shunting its resources because it's in survival mode, not memory mode," says Dr. Ressler. This is why you might be more forgetful when you are under stress or may even experience memory lapses during traumatic events.[7]

In other words, disunity consumes our brain's resources so we can't be as creative as we are when we enjoy peace and harmony in our most important relationships.

Let me ask you a few questions:

- Have you ever been nagged by stress headaches, tension pain, fatigue, an upset stomach, or sleep problems? Are you grinding your teeth at night?
- Have you been a part of an organization that had so much drama that you couldn't stop thinking about work when you were at home, but it was affecting your family relationships so much that you couldn't stop thinking about them while you were at work?

- Have you had seasons of your life characterized by increased levels of anxiety, anger, sadness, and restlessness, and an inability to concentrate? Are you in one of those seasons right now?

- Are you taking medications, or do you need medications, for anxiety and depression?

- Are your thoughts preoccupied with defending yourself (and maybe getting even) instead of being free to be creative?

- Has stress affected your most important relationships because you've been defensive and angry, or passive and disinterested?

- Is your commitment to excellence sidelined because you're preoccupied with surviving the chaos and you're afraid to endure the ridicule you'd experience from any failure?

- Do you often daydream about getting away from the chaos and being with people who are far more agreeable? . . . or maybe just getting away and being alone?

Individuals suffer when a lack of unity destroys their peace and confidence, but teams and organizations also pay a steep price for the lack of unity. When unhealthy tension becomes normal, turnover increases because people don't want to stay in a company or a church that creates (or allows) so much stress. Recruiting takes a hit because the best people steer clear of environments that bring out the worst instead of the best in their people. These organizations foster cliques and silos, with a mentality of "us versus them" between teams—and among the members of the teams because each person's daily goal is self-protection instead of using the power of unity to excel and accomplish great things. Toxic competition inflames egos, which always creates a poisonous brew of pride, fear, resentment, and envy, which produces even more division between those who receive praise or promotions and those who don't. People see their work as a steppingstone to go somewhere else instead of a vital mission they're on together. No matter how many superstars they have, these teams simply can't be as productive as those that that are unified.

Teams that lack unity are always checking each other out—to see who's getting ahead, to find fault in others, and to see if anybody is watching them. They're looking around instead of looking forward. Elite runners know that looking around and behind slows them down. It creates "drag" that hinders momentum, it distracts the runner from keeping his eyes on the finish line, and it's a clear signal to others that you're preoccupied with them. In his ten "life lessons" from running, Eric Rheam concludes, "By looking over your shoulder and allowing yourself to be distracted by the unimportant stuff, you are giving in to the lie that you are not good enough. Distracted people are folks that are not confident in what they are doing; that is why they allow themselves to get distracted so easily. Stop that and stay focused!"[8] When your head is on a swivel because you're afraid someone is going to stab you in the back, your goals change!

When I was on the totally dysfunctional church staff team, I spent countless hours venting in my journal instead of dreaming and planning a preferred future. And my mind was preoccupied with ways I could avoid spending time with others on the team, how I'd respond if "that person" said something snarky to me again, and how I could write a killer résumé so I could get out of there. (Sounds productive, doesn't it?)

NOTHING LESS

But I've seen the unstoppable power and speed of teams that are unified, and I'll never settle for anything less again. In fact, unity has become one of the seven values of our church. I'm convinced that when we get unity right, people give their very best and nothing is impossible.

The importance of unity dawned on me after I'd been on two very disunified church staff teams. The first one had five church splits in three years. Imagine being the people who were the only ones left after all the carnage! After each split, many of the kids often wanted to stay in the youth group with me while their parents looked for other churches. As you can guess, this made our pastor even more suspicious and resentful toward me. The second team was the one I described previously: we didn't like each other, and we did everything we could to avoid meaningful connections.

I believe we learn more from failures than successes, and these two painful experiences were like graduate school for me. When we started River Valley Church, I was determined to create a culture that was 180 degrees from my two previous team disasters. I was sure that if we could find a way to work together, we'd be far more productive and we'd have a blast at the same time.

At the time, I'd read plenty of books and I'd heard dozens of messages about the importance of a compelling vision, but I had a sense that we needed more than that. I didn't describe it as unity . . . at least not yet. If the vision was big enough and attractive enough, I hoped the internal motivation of the people involved would encourage creativity and dampen the temptation to bicker with each other. A lot of people were captivated by the vision of River Valley, and they gladly joined us on the journey.

From the first day, we had a basic agreement of what we were committed to be and do, and the vision propelled us to do great things. We grew, but after a few years, I realized there was something missing. The foundation of a team is trust, but we needed something beyond trust—our hearts had to be connected to enable us to work and serve as a cohesive whole. When our team was small, we functioned as a family. We cleared the air when there was conflict, we forgave each other, and we made sure we were on the same page with our plans. But when we grew so large that we couldn't have a family environment, the cohesive atmosphere deteriorated. I realized we needed to do something that still brought people together.

Unity, I understood, isn't uniformity. In the early years of our church, I had hired people who were much like me, with similar talents and personalities. As we grew, I saw big holes this management philosophy had created, and I began to hire people whose strengths and temperaments are far different from mine. It was a good move, but one day it hit me: metaphorically, half of my staff team was Mac, and the other half was PC. That was back in the day when the two platforms didn't communicate with each other, so it was a huge problem! To create and protect the unity of our team, I had to speak both languages so everyone felt understood, appreciated, and directed.

As I saw the positive results of unity on our team, I sensed God tell me, "I want you to lead like you parent." Instantly, the message made perfect sense to me. My commitment to Logan and Connor (our two sons) is to create an environment where both of them thrive, where individual strengths are celebrated—and differences are celebrated too. My purpose as their dad is to build them up, shape their characters, highlight their talents, address their failures so they learn from their mistakes, help them see that the strengths of others aren't threats to them, and encourage them to be the best they can be. That, I realized, is my role as the pastor of our church and as the leader of our staff team. It was a game-changer. (We'll come back to this concept in Chapter 9.)

MY HOPE FOR YOU

I know plenty of church and business leaders whose teams are stalled on the side of the road—and some are going in reverse, powered by suspicion, resentment, and fear. At this moment, I can see faces in my mind of people who have told me horror stories of organizations that are train wrecks. Far more leaders are settling for the speed of agreement—as long as conflict doesn't destroy production, they're fine with this speed. In the past couple of decades, however, the importance of vision has given leaders a fresh idea of what's possible. But there's more . . . always more. The speed of unity is achieved when team members care more about the organization's purpose and each other than their own acclaim. These organizations attract the best, keep the best, bring out the best, and launch the best.

I'm very much aware that there are two kinds of people reading this book. Some value unity (defined by them as a lack of tension) above every other factor in relationships, and they're suspicious of leaders who push toward a clear vision of lofty goals. They just want everyone to get along and be happy together. But others value production because they have big goals. When they've heard leaders talk about unity, it sounded like needless sentimentality that would sidetrack their bold vision . . . so they're already tempted to throw this book in the trash! Let me assure you that the call to unity isn't just a lot of tender, mushy, emotions. It's a strategy to call out the very best in each person, create a supremely positive culture, and accomplish far more than agreement and vision ever can. Leaders are shepherds, but we're shepherds with a powerful purpose.

You may be a CEO or company president, a division manager, board member, team leader, or the member of a team. You may be a pastor, staff member, or key volunteer in a local church. Or you may be a leader or a team member in a nonprofit organization. Whatever your role may be, a commitment to unity can make a difference in the lives of the people around you, and your team can be more productive.

Achieving the level of success that unity creates isn't a pipedream. I've seen it. I've felt it. My promise is that if you'll pursue the top gear, the speed of unity, you'll be a better everything: spouse, parent, friend, leader, and team member. You'll find new sources of creativity that have been overlooked because you've been preoccupied with survival. You'll be freed from the nagging compulsion to control people. You'll enjoy a deeper level of peace, and you'll truly enjoy leading and following. As you move into the highest gear, you'll find that it actually takes less effort to accomplish more because you're not fighting with people, and you're not spending time wondering how to protect yourself.

MY PROMISE IS THAT IF YOU'LL PURSUE THE TOP GEAR, THE SPEED OF UNITY, YOU'LL BE A BETTER EVERYTHING: SPOUSE, PARENT, FRIEND, LEADER, AND TEAM MEMBER.

The speed of unity may be a new concept to you, but I hope it will become second nature by the time you finish reading this book. In the next three chapters, I'll explain the sequence of increasing speeds of growth in organizations: first gear, agreement; second gear, vision; and top gear, unity.

At the end of each chapter, you'll find some questions to stimulate personal reflection and prompt lively discussions with people on your team. Don't rush through these. Take your time to think, talk, dream, and if you're so inclined, pray about how you can create and protect unity.

THINK ABOUT IT:

1. What damage have you seen (and probably experienced) on a team that is characterized by disunity?

2. So far, how would you describe "the speed of unity"?

3. What's attractive about it? What's confusing or unattractive? Do you think it's even possible?

4. From what you've read so far, which gear do you think your organization is in? Explain your answer.

5. What do you think it means to "lead like you parent"?

6. What do you hope to get out of this book?

CHAPTER 2

FIRST GEAR: THE SPEED OF AGREEMENT

The fellow that agrees with everything you say is either a fool or he is getting ready to skin you.

KIN HUBBARD

I love to drive sports cars. One day a friend loaned me his Porsche 911 convertible so I could drive with Becca to a little town in Wisconsin. From the moment I got in, it was an adrenaline rush! (I hope my friend doesn't read this book because I don't want him to know that I got his car over 100 miles an hour.) The speed and the handling were a thrill. I was one with the car—I became a Porsche 911. I felt like I could win the Grand Prix! Driving a stick shift is a ton of fun—and if you haven't learned to drive one, you gotta try it!

It doesn't matter what kind of car you drive. If it's stuck in first gear, your top speed will be only about 25 miles an hour . . . and everybody on the road will hear you coming because your engine will have a deafening whine! You spend a lot of time frantically trying to move the gear stick, but nothing seems to work. When people pass you, they look at you like you're an A1 loser, which is exactly how you feel.

At a fascinating point in the history of the Jewish people, the prophet Amos provided insight about the true condition of the nation of Israel. Their king, Jeroboam, believed he and his kingdom were doing the best they could do, but Amos saw through his foolish conclusion. The king expected the prophet to pronounce blessings, but Amos brought the devastating news that the nation of Israel was so broken and lost that in a few years it wouldn't even exist. The leaders of the nation didn't share God's design for them, so Amos asked, "Can two people walk together without agreeing on the direction?" (Amos 3:3) This was a question with a painfully obvious answer. For the nation of Israel—and for teams, companies, and churches today—"agreeing on the direction" is the first and fundamental step so they can move forward.

An agreement between at least two people is the result of discussion regarding a course of action. The parties determine that it makes sense to do something because both will benefit, and they choose to do it together. They discuss where they want to go, how they'll get there, who is responsible for each step, and when things need to happen. Or, as my friend Sam Chand crystallizes assignments of responsibility, they ask, "Who does what by when?"

Becca and I walk up to four miles several times each week. Before we leave the house early in the morning, we talk about whether we're going to walk one way to Starbucks or the other way to Caribou. (It depends on which gift card we have.) The pace of our walk gives us plenty of time, and we talk about anything and everything. These times have given us opportunities to share our hearts so we understand each other. Among countless other topics, we've discussed hard decisions we've had to make, we've brainstormed plans for trips, and, of course, we've talked about our sons and daughter-in-law.

In my previous church experiences, I was often in staff meetings when we had a lot of conversations about what was broken and needed to be fixed, and we planned for upcoming events and activities. We came to agreement about those plans, but we walked away with no more than a checklist for each person. Those conversations were the lowest common denominator for a functioning team, but we didn't have a higher, clearer, more compelling vision to inject passion into our actions, and we certainly didn't have a powerful sense of unity that propels a few teams to greatness.

When teams aren't moving at the speed of agreement, there's no measuring stick for success (or it's constantly moving) and problems multiply: people are distracted, they try to look busy to avoid criticism, they can't distinguish between what's important and what's urgent, they do as little as possible to still remain employed, they make complaining an art form, they create alliances to gang up on others they think are threats, they communicate primarily through gossip and sarcasm, they take offense at every perceived slight, and they try to make sure no one knows they spend hours each day on their fantasy football team, watching YouTube, or playing video games. They feel trapped in a meaningless eight-hour day. Their J-O-B could more accurately be spelled J-A-I-L.

THEIR J-O-B COULD MORE ACCURATELY BE SPELLED J-A-I-L.

It doesn't have to be this way, and it certainly doesn't have to stay this way. Every leader can take steps to move at the speed of agreement. It will feel like heaven on earth compared to the purgatory of being stalled or in reverse. Job descriptions and clear communication won't take a team to the speed of unity, but these tools are essential if they want to move at the speed of agreement.

If this is where you are, don't despair. There's a promise of a better future, but start where you are. If you try to start a car in third or fourth gear, it'll stall. Start in first gear, get going, then shift to second gear, and later to top gear. There's nothing wrong with driving in first gear, the speed of agreement. It's a necessary stage in gaining speed . . . especially if you've been in reverse.

HOPE AND RESISTANCE

As I've talked to leaders about the three speeds of organizations, I invariably detect an initial surge of hope. I can read their minds: "Really? Do you think our business (or church or nonprofit) can move at the speed of unity?" I assure them it's possible, but their ray of hope soon is swallowed by doubt. They may or may not actually verbalize what they're thinking: *Yeah, but what would it take?* But I can see the wheels turning. They're thinking: *Look, I'm busy enough as it is. I'm not going to spend a couple of days with HR or a coach making clay models that represent where we need to go, and when I walk out the door, we go back to doing the same things in the same way. We may feel inspired for an hour, but we're really never going to change.*

Any exciting possibilities of the future drown in today's pressing demands. I've heard plenty of excuses from leaders:

"I just don't have the right people."

"We can't afford to have anything interfere with our production schedule."

"Have you seen my team?"

"You don't understand how hard it is to work with my board."

"It'll never work here. We're limited by market share (or the economy or demographics of the community or something else)."

"We're already doing the best we can."

"Churches like ours just don't do things like that!"

Some of these leaders remind me of a parent driving the family to a vacation spot when the lofty goal is to keep the kids from tearing each other's eyes out in the backseat. Their workers feel far more grim determination than eager anticipation; far more fear than hope; far more self-doubt than confidence. Misery, they've concluded from countless painful experiences, is just the way things are. Sure, some leaders are lucky or supremely talented, but discouraged leaders only see their bad luck and the mediocre abilities of the people on their teams.

To use another metaphor, these leaders are like some coaches I've seen in youth sports. I love to coach kids, but some coaches have facial expressions like they've been convicted and sentenced to death row. They give some rudimentary directions to the kids about how to play the game, but they don't inspire anyone. Their idea of "a team" is basic compliance to their grim instructions. And in fact, as the game progresses and their players make mistakes, they bark at the kids with obvious contempt . . . or they don't even notice because they're on their phones. The coaches' real goal is to get the game over as soon as possible so they can go home. They don't invest their hearts in the kids to teach them, inspire them, and help them learn from their mistakes.

Sadly, a lot of leaders, parents, and coaches believe they're doing everything they can do for the people around them, but they're not. Agreement is all they've ever dreamed of, and they have no conception of moving at the speeds of vision and unity.

AT LEAST

Organizations simply can't function without basic ground rules and clear expectations. The relationship between the leader and the team is transactional: both give something valuable to get something they want. Employees are putting in their time, making sales, serving food, and doing what's expected so they can get a paycheck. They operate on the basis of job descriptions, and many people give as little of themselves as possible to get the benefits they signed up for. The speed of agreement is often based on transactions like this:

- Position details: general information about the job
- List of responsibilities: the boss's expectations
- Reporting structure: who is responsible for the person's production
- Compensation: salary and benefits

WHEN I EXPLAIN THE THREE SPEEDS, SOMETIMES PEOPLE WAIT UNTIL OTHERS HAVE LEFT, AND WHISPER, "PASTOR ROB, WHAT CAN I DO IF MY TEAM ISN'T EVEN AT THE SPEED OF AGREEMENT?"

Now, didn't that just make your heart soar? Of course not. The speed of agreement is essential as a starting point, but it doesn't inspire anyone. Bosses that rely too heavily on job descriptions have the advantage of making expectations clear, but they severely limit the team members' passion, creativity, and effectiveness. In a dynamic, fast-changing culture, rigid expectations can become outdated, and they don't encourage people to uncover their best ideas and think "outside the box."

When I explain the three speeds, sometimes people wait until others have left, and whisper, "Pastor Rob, what can I do if my team isn't even at the speed of agreement?" Some of them are team leaders, and I encourage them to take steps to clarify the terms of agreement, and if someone on the team demonstrates he isn't in agreement, make the hard decision to invite him to find other employment. But many of the people who ask this question are team members who are suffering under poor leadership, with bosses like the dad driving his family on vacation or the grumpy coach who didn't want the role in the first place. These team members have two options: If they're convinced the culture is irreparably toxic and change won't happen no matter how many promises are made, they should look for another company or church with another team that's moving at least at the speed of agreement. The other option is to remain and become "a virus of vision," infecting other team members with the joy of supporting each other, quickly resolving conflict, and affirming each person's contribution to the team. Sooner or later, the leader may realize this person is having a very positive impact on the team members . . . and on the production of the team. It's possible that this leader will be so impressed that he shifts into a different gear.

I've talked to team leaders who work in a company that's stuck in neutral on the side of the road. They have to play by their boss's game plan, but they exercise enough freedom to create a positive environment for their teams. They live in the constant tension between a stagnant culture in the company and the dynamic, creative, positive atmosphere they're trying to build into their teams. Every day, they swim upstream against the current of the company's pessimism and lethargy, but they keep swimming and taking their teams with them. These brave leaders are my heroes.

GETTING IN GEAR

We can learn a lot from leaders in different fields about transactions at the speed of agreement:

Sports

On youth sports teams, most of the kids are excited to be on the team, and they're willing to do anything to get to play. Agreement means they show up on time, they take instruction, they play hard, they have fun, they understand the position they play, everybody gets in the game, and they play as a team (which means if it's basketball, they actually pass the ball to kids who are open). Smart coaches spell all this out at the first practice, and they follow through with these commitments. But I've also tried to coach a few kids that didn't even want to be there. Their parents forced them to join, and it didn't take a psychologist to read the child's body language and facial expressions. The parents were in agreement with each other, but they forgot to bring their child into the conversation.

Business

A commitment to the speed of agreement can happen anywhere, and when it's present, it can lead to much bigger things.

If you think you're stuck and hopeless, look at the turnaround of Mike Pisciotta. When he was eighteen, he almost overdosed on Xanax. When he woke up, he wasn't in the hospital; he was in prison. He had robbed two stores, was tried and convicted, and he was sentenced to ten years in prison in Florida. Still, he refused to give up. He wanted to make something of himself instead of getting swallowed by the emptiness and bitterness of prison life. He checked out business books from the prison library, especially ones on marketing, because he was determined to become an entrepreneur. The prison environment wasn't supportive. He remembers, "I felt like a crab desperately fighting to get out of a bucket. And all of the other crabs . . . the inmates and the officers, were desperately fighting to pull me back in. Officers would shake down my cell and confiscate any books that I didn't have a receipt for. And they'd do this purely out of spite."

Mike struggled to stay positive, but it was really hard in that hostile environment. A few years into his sentence, he met another inmate, Tyrone. Both were committed to turn their lives around, and Mike was amazed at Tyrone's talent for languages. In only a few months, Tyrone taught Mike to be fluent in Spanish. As a budding entrepreneur, Mike decided to charge other inmates for language lessons. They paid him in Ramen noodles and tuna packets. Other prisoners and the officers were very suspicious of anyone who colored outside the lines, and Mike was tagging the whole prison! He explains, "I was making money, but I also attracted a lot of negative attention from people who frowned on attempts at self-improvement. My constant learning was often interpreted as a statement that I thought I was better than everybody else. For the most part I brushed it off. I'd always been confident in my abilities, borderline arrogant. But I didn't learn new skills to show off, I learned them to stand a better chance of surviving life outside of prison after my release."

Tyrone wasn't Mike's only source of encouragement. A local church youth leader, Robin, had a popular weekly radio show. Mike had become a Christian, and he enjoyed listening to Robin every Friday night. Mike asked his mother to call the station and tell Robin that he loved her show, and Mike began writing her letters. She was impressed with his passion for Scripture. When they finally met, she wore a T-shirt that said, "I Wanna Be Like Mike."

The two became friends, and the relationship continued to grow. Six weeks after Mike was released, they got married. As he feared, he had a hard time finding steady employment. He interviewed for good jobs, but when companies learned about his record, they passed. Soon, Robin was pregnant, and when the local economy went south in 2009 during the Great Recession, her small business failed. Desperate, they drove around neighborhoods at night picking up printers, computers, and televisions that were out for the next day's trash pickup. They sold them on Craigslist to make ends meet.

While he was in prison, Mike had been isolated from incredible advances in technology, but now he was making up for the delay in his learning curve. He and Robin started an online business to create websites for marketing and sales. Robin recalls, "We started turning our clients into millionaires. Eventually we had a waiting list of people who wanted to work with us and we could choose who we did business with." Mike and Robin's success came at a steep cost in time they had to devote to their clients. For a while, they were almost crushed by the pressure, but they eventually found ways to balance their time and responsibilities.

When we look at Mike's story through the lens of the three speeds, we see that his life was going backwards . . . in a hurry when he was put in prison, but he found the courage to take small steps of agreement with Tyrone, and those steps led to success no one else in his prison could have imagined. He began with simple transactions, trading Spanish lessons for noodles and tuna. Success breeds success, and Robin became his next partner as they agreed on a better future for both of them. The path wasn't smooth or easy. In fact, it was uphill all the way, but an agreement with a friend and a life partner made all the difference.[9]

Mike was determined to go above and beyond, but many employees expect to fulfill only the minimum requirement. Chris Lind is a friend of mine who often interviews prospective employees for his company, and he told me many of them want to know where the limits are, and more importantly, what they can get away with. They regularly ask questions like: "How many days can I be absent and still keep my job?" and "How late can someone be and get only a warning?" Chris told me that he'd like to hire me to be an undercover employee for a day. He wants me to push all the limits, cross all the boundaries, and be as worthless as possible. Then he'd come in, call me out, and yell, "You're lazy! You're fired!" (I'm not sure why he thinks I'd be perfect for this role.) He said, "A lot of people who join our company believe they were created for their jobs, and they're a joy to lead. But historically, the ones that are here only for a paycheck . . . they were killing me."

Frankly, I can't understand people who are only transactional. When I was young, my grandfather told me, "When you ask for a job, tell them, 'If you hire me, I'll be the best employee you've ever had. After a week, if you don't like my work, you can fire me and I won't take a penny. I'll show you how valuable I can be to your company.'" This attitude has impressed my employers from my high school days until today.

But I have to admit, as a student, I did the minimum to pass courses. In fact, I spent time calculating what I had to make on a final exam so I could pass. For one final exam, I walked into the classroom, filled in multiple choice questions at random, signed my name to the test, and handed it in as the other students were just getting started. The professor looked at me as if to say, "What do you think you're doing? You can't be that flippant with my exam!" But I had calculated that I could make a zero on the final and still come out with a B in the course, so I didn't study, I didn't take time to think about my answers, and I wasn't concerned about what the prof thought of me. (Don't let my sons read this part.)

Churches

When a church is moving at the speed of agreement, people are involved only on the best days and the worst days. The best days are Christmas, Easter, and weddings; the worst days are sickness and death of members of the church. The pastor has an implicit agreement with the people in the church, especially the volunteers: "I'll push you, but only to the point that you push back. At that point, I'll pull back. I'm not willing to put up with any tension." The church exists, but it doesn't grow. People attend because it's comfortable and doesn't require much of them, not because they share a common purpose to make a difference. Oh, a handful of people are activists—they volunteer because it feels good and they benefit from the involvement, but an equal handful are antagonists and find fault with everything. The two groups are small, and they balance each other out . . . usually.

BEYOND AGREEMENT

Transactional businesses can keep their doors open if they provide good enough products or services to customers who don't want to drive too far. But with services like Amazon Prime, convenience is on each person's doorstep the next day. Businesses that don't evolve, market themselves adequately, and keep refining their products run the risk of being stampeded by ones with a clearer vision and message.

BUSINESSES THAT DON'T EVOLVE, MARKET THEMSELVES ADEQUATELY, AND KEEP REFINING THEIR PRODUCTS RUN THE RISK OF BEING STAMPEDED BY ONES WITH A CLEARER VISION AND MESSAGE.

And a lot of people are leaving churches that haven't advanced past agreement. They hear about plenty of churches that are doing great things, churches that have a powerful vision and a sense of unity, and they aren't satisfied with the minimum. Years ago, before the Internet transformed how we see the world, transactional churches could survive, but in the past couple of decades, the emphasis on vision has captured the hearts of countless leaders and followers.

Agreement is a necessary starting point, but it's not enough. There's more.

THINK ABOUT IT:

1. Have you ever driven (or ridden in) a car that was stuck in first gear? What was it like?
2. Does your organization use job descriptions? How are they helpful?
3. Do job descriptions stimulate or limit creativity and cross-pollination of ideas? Explain your answer.

4. What are some reasons agreement is necessary, at least as a first gear, for a team or an organization?

5. Why do you think some people are satisfied with staying at this speed? What's the perceived payoff for remaining there?

6. Are you satisfied with this speed? Explain your answer.

CHAPTER 3

SECOND GEAR: THE SPEED OF VISION

If you are working on something exciting that you really care about, you don't have to be pushed. The vision pulls you.

STEVE JOBS

When we started River Valley Church, I was determined that we wouldn't have the same corrosive blend of fighting, blaming, and toxic passivity I'd experienced in the previous two churches where I'd served. The toxic environment had sucked the life out of the staff teams, and it had sucked the life out of me, but I was determined: "Never again!" I had read books and listened to brilliant speakers in the business and church worlds, and I was convinced a powerful vision was the ultimate solution to organizational problems . . . the top gear. Like many other leaders, I wondered if the ability to cast vision was an innate talent or a learned skill. I soon realized it's both. It was second nature to me to dream and communicate a picture of a preferred future to the people on our team and in our church, and they ate it up. But I could always find ways to improve.

I had to figure out how to communicate our vision so it inspired people instead of either making them laugh at the absurdity of it or having them conclude that I had lost my mind. (Those may be the same thing!) I had to bring people along at their pace. Some were immediately excited about the biggest ideas, but others couldn't get on board until I explained all the steps involved. The vision helped us organize our planning and focus our resources on what's most important. It generated tremendous enthusiasm, which tapped into the passions of everyone involved, attracted the participation of people who had been on the sidelines, and led to accelerated growth. In all of this, we met or exceeded the goals of our primary metrics: changed lives, leadership development, and serving people in need.

I worked hard on making the vision crystal clear, assuring people that accomplishing it was possible and reminding them that the challenge would bring out their talents. I promised that in the end, the hard work and prayer would be completely worth it because we would see a huge difference in countless people's lives.

From Day 1, our vision was to grow to a church of 1000 people, give $250,000 each year to world missions, provide housing for visiting missionaries, and plant churches. That was it—just four parts—but it stretched us to trust God, stay focused, and work like crazy. The vision included several intangibles.: We weren't going to be transactional. We were going beyond the speed of agreement to inspire people to give their best. And we were going to be a contemporary church that reaches young adults, values ministry to children, and is committed to excellence.

But what if . . .? What if one or more people on our launch team wasn't even at the speed of agreement? I've known plenty of leaders who would have thought, *Well, at least I have some warm bodies. Maybe that person will change.* Yeah, it's possible, but it's unlikely. I knew that the first shoots would establish the direction of our tree, so I wasn't willing to include anyone who wasn't at least with us at the speed of agreement. This meant they were on board with their particular role and responsibilities, the reporting structure, and accountability. But I wanted to move much faster than the speed of agreement. From the very start, I pointed our team to a culture and a strategy that propelled us at the speed of vision.

FROM THE VERY START, I POINTED OUR TEAM TO A CULTURE AND A STRATEGY THAT PROPELLED US AT THE SPEED OF VISION.

To be honest, at the beginning I oversold the vision, and a lot of people laughed. They rolled their eyes and smiled—not a happy, positive smile, but more of a smirk, as if to say, "Yeah, sure. We've heard all this before. Get a life, Rob!" We had a big vision but few resources. In fact, not long after we started, I'd spent every dime and maxed out my credit cards. Becca and I were $100,000 in debt. If anyone had reason to doubt, it was Becca, but she was my biggest cheerleader. (Since those days, I've learned a few things about planting churches!)

The resistance hit close to home. When I told Becca's dad my vision for the church, he leaned back and said, "Whoa, whoa, whoa. I think a really good vision is to grow enough so you can be paid a salary." He paused to let it sink in, and then he told me, "Rob, I think that would be a really good goal." (Later, when the church grew to 200 and I was actually receiving a salary, he smiled and told me, "You did it!" When we were at 400, he exclaimed, "Wow! Way to go!" At 1000, he shook his head and asked, "What's going on at the church?" What he meant was, "I'm shocked!" When we grew to almost 2000, he drew a different conclusion: "Rob, I don't know how the church has grown so much. You're really not that smart." At 4000, he told people, "I taught Rob all he knows! That's why he married my daughter.")

Recently, Becca remembered our conversations when we started the church. She reminded me, "You told people that our church would own houses where missionaries could live when they were on furlough. I thought you were crazy because you and I didn't even own *a* house!"

As I learned to communicate the vision more clearly, I could see the lights come on in people's minds. They wanted to be part of something much bigger than themselves, they appreciated having clear goals, and they were excited (or relieved) when we outlined the steps to get there. I had hoped a powerful vision would propel our team and our church, and I was seeing growth played out in front of me every day. We attracted people who wanted their lives to count, who were visionaries who had been frustrated with the lack of vision where they'd been before. Soon, I didn't have to push at all. In fact, their energy was pushing me along.

Let's take a closer look at what vision is and what it does for the leader and the organization.

WHAT IT IS

The concept of organizational vision has been inherent in leaders' minds since the dawn of time, but it has taken center stage in the last few decades. One of the first companies to create a vision statement was Sony in the 1970s. Soon, Apple began to communicate a clear statement about their future goals. One of the first definitions of vision was penned by James M. Kouzes and Barry Z. Pozner in *The Leadership Challenge*: vision is "an ideal and unique image of the future."[10] Soon, the dam broke and leaders in every field were talking about the importance of vision. The concept was considered as important as benchmarking and strategic planning.[11]

I'm not sure what took our modern and postmodern culture so long to see that vision is crucial for every organization. About twenty-six centuries ago, the prophet Habakkuk was tasked with standing guard over God's people. He felt the responsibility deep in his soul, and he trusted God to give him clear direction. The Lord gave him this instruction:

> "Write my answer plainly on tablets,
> so that a runner can carry the correct message to others.
> This vision is for a future time.
> It describes the end, and it will be fulfilled.
> If it seems slow in coming, wait patiently,
> for it will surely take place.
> It will not be delayed." (Habakkuk 2:2-3)

The vision wasn't just about the moment; it was about the future. It wasn't just for the prophet; it was for everybody. It wouldn't happen quickly, but God promised that it would eventually be fulfilled. Isn't that the framework of the kind of vision that propels leaders in every kind of organization?

I could list literally thousands of leaders' insights about vision, but let me point to just a few. They come from business, the church, the arts, sports, and entertainment. Vision is important everywhere!

The greatest danger for most of us is not that our aim is too high and we miss it, but that it is too low and we reach it.

—MICHELANGELO

Someone is sitting in the shade today because someone planted a tree long ago.

—*WARREN BUFFETT*

A clear vision, backed by definite plans, gives you a tremendous feeling of confidence and personal power.

—*BRIAN TRACY*

Dreams are extremely important. You can't do it unless you can imagine it.

—*GEORGE LUCAS*

The only limits are, as always, those of vision.

—*JAMES BROUGHTON*

Keep your dreams alive. Understand to achieve anything requires faith and belief in yourself, vision, hard work, determination, and dedication. Remember all things are possible for those who believe.

—*GAIL DEVERS*

Success is about dedication. You may not be where you want to be or do what you want to do when you're on the journey. But you've got to be willing to have vision and foresight that leads you to an incredible end.

—*USHER*

People buy into the leader before they buy into the vision.

—*JOHN C. MAXWELL*

Vision gets the dreams started. Dreaming employs your God-given imagination to reinforce the vision. Both are part of something I believe is absolutely necessary to building the life of a champion, a winner, a person of high character who is consistently at the top of whatever game he or she is in.

—EMMITT SMITH

One of my favorite quotes is by Simon Sinek: "Great leaders must have two things: a vision of the world that does not yet exist and the ability to communicate that vision clearly." We may use the terms "dream" and "vision" interchangeably, but in *Visioneering,* pastor Andy Stanley identifies important differences between leaders who have dreams and those who have a vision: "Dreamers dream about things being different. Visionaries envision themselves making a difference. Dreamers think about how nice it would be for something to be done. Visionaries look for an opportunity to do something."[12]

WHEN I'M PREPARING TO COMMUNICATE A PICTURE OF A BETTER FUTURE, I INSTINCTIVELY ASK MYSELF THESE QUESTIONS: "WHERE ARE WE NOW?" "WHERE CAN WE GO?" AND "WHAT WILL IT TAKE TO GET THERE?"

When I'm preparing to communicate a picture of a better future, I instinctively ask myself these questions: "Where are we now?" "Where can we go?" and "What will it take to get there?" I see my role as a cavalry scout in a Western movie. He leaves the soldiers and rides ahead to see what's true and what's possible. When he comes back, he reports what he's seen, and he makes recommendations about the best route to get to their destination. He explains where the enemy is hidden, how to avoid them or attack them, and where to find resources along the way. The history of warfare shows the vital importance of a scout's information, and the devastation an army suffers without it. As our church's scout, I "ride ahead" as I imagine the future and consider all the questions about what needs to happen to get there.

Of course, the scout hasn't seen every obstacle and danger. The cavalry has to be alert as they follow his directions so they aren't caught off guard. As he rides with them, he knows he doesn't have to meet the challenges alone. In the same way, it's a leader's job to scout the future, but when he rides with the team, they provide insight and resources to overcome problems the scout had foreseen as well as those he hadn't anticipated.

WHAT IT DOES

For leaders, insomnia results from two different causes: some of us can't sleep because we're so worried about managing all the craziness on our teams, but others can't sleep because we're so excited about our opportunities. When people have a vision, they get out of bed each morning with a spring in their step. They anticipate the adventures they'll face that day. I've known a lot of leaders who are more like Eeyore than Winnie the Pooh or Christopher Robin, but I almost always look at the future through the lens of possibilities. When the vision for our church was fresh, sleep seemed like an interference. I wanted to spend all day every day (and all night) accomplishing things to fulfill the vision. (I actually tried to see if I could get by on four hours of sleep, but my doctor talked me out of that idea.)

A vision gives clarity to the leader and the team. They usually don't have to choose between the good and the bad, but they always have to choose between the good, the better, and the best. Vision helps them see what's best so they can pour their hearts and resources into the things that matter most. People who have a vision are far more creative because they realize what they create will have a big impact.

Money follows vision. A lot of leaders won't even talk about a better future until they have money in the bank, but they don't understand the sequence of cause and effect. When leaders cast vision, people with resources want to get behind it, and they become very generous. Usually, money problems are actually vision problems.

Another difference between dreams and visions is that dreams are often huge and amorphous, like "ending world hunger," but visions necessarily become concrete: we do these things with these people with these resources to reach these intermediate benchmarks on the way to fulfill our ultimate aim. A workable vision to feed the hungry might involve a specific geographic area, the acquisition of resources (such as leftover food from restaurants or food pantry donations), a means of distribution to the people who need them, the manpower to make this happen, with a schedule and intermediate goals to show progress.

Does a compelling vision reduce or increase conflict on the team? Yes, both. On a team that's going somewhere, conflict is completely different. Vision reduces interpersonal tension because everyone is working together to accomplish something bigger than themselves, but passionate, creative people have ideas, and their drive sometimes causes them to bump up against others on the team who have similar drives but different ideas. In my experience, most of the conflict that happens in the context of a powerful vision is "iron sharpening iron," not a sledgehammer bludgeoning concrete. In other words, rubbing up against others' ideas makes people think more clearly and prompts them to be more creative and more willing to appreciate others' input.

THE PRICE WE PAY

People who insist on every aspect of their lives being safe and carefully controlled don't allow themselves to be inspired by a big vision of the future. Vision requires us to live, at least to some degree, in the "what ifs" and the "not yets." Those who are fearful don't want to be stretched because they don't want to fail and look foolish. The fact is that none of us want to fail and look foolish, but the cost of passivity is far higher than the risk of occasionally being wrong. And the benefits of passivity are far lower than the rewards of being on a team with people who are committed to do something great for others.

When we began at River Valley and I cast the vision for our church, we got very mixed responses: about a third were supercharged and ready to go, about a third were interested but wanted some assurances, and the rest were skeptical of anything that wasn't familiar to them. My responses were equally varied: I was thrilled to invest time to equip the first group, I was eager to answer questions the second group asked (but to be honest, I was more than a little impatient with some of them), and I felt that I always had to look over my shoulder to anticipate the subtle and not-so-subtle attacks by the skeptics.

After years of successes, however, the vast majority of the people we've attracted and kept are excited when I cast a new vision. They've seen incredible things happen before, so they're confident the latest idea will accomplish even more great things. Over the years, they've grown to trust me, and now they trust that the direction I tell them we need to go is the right one.

But the path to fulfillment of a vision is never a straight line. Some people say that visons have a predictable life cycle: birth, death, and resurrection. The death of the idea may happen for many reasons, but it's always excruciating. Very often, though, it comes back at a different time, perhaps in a different form, and with a clearer focus. Andy Stanley describes the down time as a desert, a time of emptiness and loneliness that all leaders suffer, but it never gets easy. He writes, "So what's the deal with the desert? I don't know. But I do know the time between catching a glimpse of what God wants to do through us and the time when we are led to move out often feels like a desert experience. The desert always feels like a complete waste of time. It is only when we are able to look back that our desert experiences make sense."[13]

We also pay a price as we live in the tension between staying sharp and staying humble. The minds of visionaries are always humming. We can think of a zillion ideas, and when we land on one that rings right, we spend countless hours refining the concept, planning the process, determining the best way to communicate it, and anticipating responses. In all this, it's easy for us to conclude that our idea is the best one anyone has ever had! Yes, it's probably a really good idea, but no, it's almost certainly not unique. We can tell if we're humble by how willing we are to listen to others' ideas, how much we incorporate their ideas into the vision, and how much credit we give them.

HOW TO GET A VISION, HOW TO CLARIFY ONE

I know a young man who planted a church in another part of the country. In the first year, he cast a clear vision for the church's initial season of growth, and people were excited. When they reached their goal, his people asked, "So, what's your vision for the next year?" He was stumped. The entire first year, he had been focused only on what needed to happen today, this week, this month, and this year. He hadn't spent time imagining where the church could go when they met their first benchmark. He had borrowed his vision from his previous church experience, but he hadn't learned how to generate and articulate one on his own.

I have two suggestions about crafting your picture of the future: First, expose yourself to leaders who have a strong, clear vision. You might read their books, listen to their podcasts, go to their conferences, or ask them to mentor you. Be a sponge. Soak up everything they can offer you, and ask great questions to figure out how to lead your business, church, or nonprofit.

IF THERE'S BEEN ANY "SECRET" TO MY LEADERSHIP, IT'S THAT I'VE BORROWED THE INSIGHTS AND EXPERIENCES OF GIFTED PEOPLE.

If there's been any "secret" to my leadership, it's that I've borrowed the insights and experiences of gifted people. Not long after we began River Valley, I wanted to go to a John Maxwell event, but like all church plants, we were really short on funds. The cost, about $2000 for the trip and the event, wouldn't have been more daunting if it had been a million dollars, but I realized I couldn't afford *not* to go. The benefit of learning from one of the most gifted leaders in the world was well worth it. Over the years, I've refined our church's vision many times, and each one is bigger and more specific than the last. When I look back at these revisions, I remember the impact of particular people who spoke into my life at that time. I'm deeply indebted to them.

Second, imagine yourself as a cavalry scout in a time-travel sci-fi. Ride out into the future—one year, three years, five years, and ten years—and see what's on the hills in the distance. (I don't think it's helpful to go past ten years. That's plenty far enough for this scout!) I let the vision of five years shape the steppingstones of the years up to that point, and I spend time thinking through the specific intermediate goals, along with the resources and people it will take to meet them.

EGO OR MISSION?

In Jim Collins's extensive study of companies in *Good to Great,* he saw that the leaders of great companies were different from other CEOs. He identifies five different levels of leadership and describes a Level 5 Leader as "an individual who blends extreme personal humility with intense professional will. We found leaders of this type at the helm of every good-to-great company . . . they were self-effacing individuals who displayed the fierce resolve to do whatever needed to be done to make the company great."[14]

The speed of vision moves the focus from *me* to *us*, and in fact, from *us* to *them*. We're no longer transactional in the speed of agreement, doing our work for a personal payoff. And the leader isn't doing it to be invited to speak at the next conference or to be written up in *Inc.* or a denominational magazine. We have drive, but our passion is other-directed; we're ambitious, but so that others may flourish. As Jim Collins explains, leaders who are moving at the speed of vision "are a study in duality: modest and willful, humble and fearless."[15]

At the speed of vision, we encounter a lot of bumps in the road, and we have to put out a lot of fires. If the speed of agreement is walking, the speed of vision is running. For years, I didn't know there was a higher gear, but there is: the speed of unity. That's when we're flying.

THINK ABOUT IT:

1. How would you describe the differences between the speed of agreement and the speed of vision?

2. What are some benefits of "writing the vision" and using the writing process to refine it? How does it help the leader? How does it help the team? How does it help the rest of the organization and the customers or attenders?

3. Have you been in an organization that had (or has) a clear, compelling vision? If you have, how did it affect you and the people around you? If you haven't, what have you missed?

4. What are some reasons people might be wary of a leader who has a bold vision for the company, church, or nonprofit? What can the leader do to address those fears?

5. How should a leader relate to each group of people across the spectrum of responses: those who are instantly excited and jump on board, those who are hesitant until they see more details, and those who find fault with the plan and refuse to get on the train?

6. Are you happy with your team's vision of the future? Explain your answer.

CHAPTER 4

TOP GEAR: THE SPEED OF UNITY

In order to have a winner, the team must have a feeling of unity; every player must put the team first—ahead of personal glory.

PAUL "BEAR" BRYANT

The Porsche 911 . . . 100 miles an hour . . . "being one" with the car and the road . . . I love it! Organizations that move at the speed of unity are wonderfully exhilarating . . . and quite rare. I don't know very much about Formula 1 and NASCAR racing, but I know this: the owners, drivers, and mechanics spend a lot of time fine-tuning the engine and the aerodynamics to squeeze yet another mile per hour out of the car's performance. The work they do before the race and in the pits enables the cars to run at incredible speeds and handle turns with grace and precision. Everyone involved plays a vital role. In the winner's circle, the driver is in the spotlight and gets the cheers, but drivers know they can't win without the seamless and passionate efforts of every person on the team.

At the speed of agreement, leaders are looking for compliance with the stated expectations (and as we've said, for some leaders and their teams, this is a monumental step forward). At the speed of vision, leaders build a team that is dedicated to fulfilling a bold mission. At the speed of unity, leaders create an environment where people bring out the best in each other—it's no longer just about the leader relating to each team member, it's about the team members encouraging, supporting, and sharpening each other.

When I've talked to groups about the speed of unity, some have asked, "What's wrong with the speed of vision? It seems pretty good to me!" It depends on where you're coming from. If you've plodded along at the speed of agreement, the speed of vision is thrilling. But when you get a glimpse of the speed of unity, second gear doesn't look quite so attractive anymore.

Unity isn't a luxury; it's crucial. Many passages in the Bible encourage people to pursue the power of unity, yet warn that while it's precious, it's also fragile. Not long after Jesus died, was raised from the dead, and ascended back into heaven, the fledgling church was under attack by the same religious authorities who conspired with the Romans to kill Him. For those believers, unity was essential for support and resources, and in some cases, it was a matter of life or death. The historian Luke tells us, "All the believers were united in heart and mind" (Acts 4:32). A few years later, another leader in the early Christian movement, Paul, wrote a letter to a group of believers. He began with some rhetorical questions that, to them and us, have obvious answers: "Is there any encouragement from belonging to Christ? Any comfort from his love? Any fellowship together in the Spirit? Are your hearts tender and compassionate?" Then he gave them clear instructions about what it takes to create and maintain unity: "Then make me truly happy by agreeing wholeheartedly with each other, loving one another, and working together with one mind and purpose. Don't be selfish; don't try to impress others. Be humble, thinking of others as better than yourselves. Don't look out only for your own interests, but take an interest in others, too." But Paul wasn't quite finished. He told them to look at the ultimate example of someone whose humility and courage created loyal relationships: "You must have the same attitude that Christ Jesus had" (Philippians 2:1-5).

Unity isn't a pipedream. It can be a reality as leaders and followers experience security, which then enables them to reach out instead of pull back, to listen instead of defend, and to value instead of compete. When it happens, it's incredibly beautiful and powerful. It's literally a taste of heaven on earth.

WHEN IT HAPPENS, IT'S INCREDIBLY BEAUTIFUL AND POWERFUL. IT'S LITERALLY A TASTE OF HEAVEN ON EARTH.

IT'S LIKE THIS . . .

As I've mentioned, people often ask me, "Pastor Rob, how has your church grown so big, and how does your staff team run so fast?" Great teachers often use similes and metaphors to connect with their audience. Let me use illustrations of the "magic" of racecars and flocks of migrating birds.

If you watch a NASCAR race for more than a minute or two, you notice that the cars are really close to each other, front to back. They're using a technique called *drafting,* which saves fuel by minimizing aerodynamic drag on the following car. In "How NASCAR Drafting Works," Eric Baxter explains:

> If you think you can pilot a NASCAR race car around Alabama's Talladega Superspeedway at 180 miles per hour (290 kilometers per hour) with more than 40 of your closest friends and enemies hot on your tail, you'd better think again. It takes more than a lead foot and nerves of steel. It's all about guts and brains and ability—and one of the most critical abilities is understanding the draft, or as many drivers put it, "seeing the air."
>
> Drafting is a game of small numbers and risky strategy playing out in a larger drama. Good drafting can turn a humdrum race into a real humdinger and a bumper-to-bumper slugfest into high-speed chess and produce the kinds of races that are talked about for years afterward.
>
> When the lead car rockets down the track it pushes through the air leaving a disturbed, or "dirty," wake behind it. The second car can slip into that disturbed air stream and reap the benefits—that is, if the driver is talented.[16]

In a race, it's common to see several cars lined up only inches apart as they fly around the track. That's a picture of the speed of unity. The drivers are taking advantage of others' efforts, and the result is maximum performance for everybody. Drafting is both an art and a science. It takes talent and finesse to get the most out of drafting, and only the best drivers can do it with excellence.

In the spring and fall, most of us get a chance to see one of the wonders of unity in nature: flocks of geese and ducks flying in a V formation. Most of us remember from our grade school science class that the birds do this to conserve energy. However, *National Geographic* reports a study that discovered the ballet of the birds is much more intricate than anyone previously guessed. The birds, as you may have noticed, are uniformly spaced about three feet apart. The report explains that the power of the formation comes from the precise movement and synchronization of the wings. The study, led by Steven Portugal at a British school of veterinary medicine, found that the formation doesn't hold the real magic. The report explains Portugal's discovery:

> But flying in a V isn't just about staying in the right place. It's also about *flapping at the right time.* As each bird flaps its wings, the trail of upwash left by its wingtips also moves up and down. The birds behind can somehow sense this and adjust their own flapping to keep their own wings within this moving zone of free lift. "They trace the same path that the bird in front traced through the air," explains Portugal.

Portugal and his team made other discoveries: They expected the efficiency of coordinated flapping to be about twenty percent, but it was much higher. And when the birds change positions, their wing motions often get out of sequence, but they change their flapping to adjust and get back in rhythm. It had been assumed that the birds learned their skills from older birds, but the study found that they learned from each other: each bird in the formation contributed to the success of all the others. The study concludes:

> How do they manage? No one knows. The easiest answer is that they're just watching the bird in front and beating their wings accordingly. They might be using their wing feathers to sense the air flow around them. Or they could just be relying on simple positive feedback. "They're flying around, they hit a

spot that feels good, and they think: Oh, hey, if I flap like this, it's easier," says Portugal.[17]

These birds have perfected the skills necessary for the speed of unity. One of the things to remember is that the entire flock has a single goal: to fly north in the spring for mating season and fly south in the fall for milder weather. We may have assumed they were moving at the speed of vision (the clear goal of saving energy), but they actually are moving at the speed of unity (carefully choreographed flapping). From a distance, their pattern of flight looks simple, but the study found the secret to their success is the intricate coordination of their efforts.

That's what the speed of unity looks like on our teams, too. When we're in alignment with each other, we're skillfully drafting on each other so we conserve energy and move faster and farther, and we're flapping our wings in carefully orchestrated ways to help each other contribute to the team's success. I'm reminded of the motto of the Three Musketeers: "All for one and one for all." That's the speed of unity. When people interview for a job at River Valley, they're often afraid they can't run as fast as they see us running. I tell them, "We go much faster than you realize, but it's much easier than you think. It's because we're all aligned."

CULTURE IS EVERYTHING

Businesses, churches, and nonprofits are realizing that having people aligned with the culture of the organization is more important than a brilliant strategy, a killer marketing campaign, and plenty of resources. For employees, competence is important, but alignment with the culture is crucial. Agreement is foundational, and vision defines the purpose and coordinates the roles, but unity is both the glue and the oil: glue that holds people together in the good times and bad, and oil that enables them to work together with minimal friction as they pursue the purpose. In the speed of unity, the important thing isn't just *what we're doing*; it's *who we're becoming* as a team and an organization. In a transaction, people are in it for the personal payoff; in a vision, they're committed to accomplish a goal bigger than themselves; and with unity, success is a shared commodity.

BUSINESSES, CHURCHES, AND NONPROFITS ARE REALIZING THAT HAVING PEOPLE ALIGNED WITH THE CULTURE OF THE ORGANIZATION IS MORE IMPORTANT THAN A BRILLIANT STRATEGY, A KILLER MARKETING CAMPAIGN, AND PLENTY OF RESOURCES.

In hundreds of conversations with leaders over the years, it's my guess that twenty percent of organizations live in constant chaos, about fifty percent function at the minimal level at the speed of agreement, twenty-five percent have found the key of vision, and only five percent are in the sweet spot running at the speed of unity. And even for those few, many of the leaders can't really explain what they're doing that's galvanizing their teams into a powerful unit. They have an intuitive sense of how to create a dynamic, supportive culture . . . and it shows, even if they can't articulate it.

In my conversations about the speed of unity, some leaders have told me, "That's what I've been creating, but I didn't have the language for it until I heard you." They're already in the five percent. And others have almost shouted, "That's what I want!" But almost instantly, the look on their face changes, and they ask, "What do I have to do to get my team up to the speed of unity?" They remember how hard it was to shift gears from the speed of agreement to the speed of vision, and they're worried that the next shift will be too costly. They've sweat blood and invested virtually all their leadership capital to get to vision, and they don't think they have much left.

I assure them that my efforts to align the team around unity isn't as big a jump as it was from agreement to vision. They people on the team are already on board with the purpose and the plan, and the vast majority of them are excited about being on a mutually supportive team. They also like the idea of getting more done with less conflict and fewer fires to put out!

THREE SHIFTS

My optimism about the shift to top gear isn't just Rob-speak; it's perfectly reasonable. The move from a toxic culture to agreement is excruciating. Leaders have to change their standards, enforce those standards, and weather the inevitable backlash from the malcontents . . . before firing them. Finding competent new hires is difficult because the word on the street is that the organization is a terrible place to work, so the best people steer clear. It often takes enormous effort and significant time to make the first shift, but leaders pay an exorbitant price if they chicken out.

The shift from agreement to vision is easier, but it's still difficult. When a fresh, bold vision is cast, we uncover the real motivations of people around us. Some, we're glad to see, are thrilled to invest their lives in a great cause (and they wonder what took us so long). But others shrug their shoulders or roll their eyes. They ask questions like, "Will I have to do even more work than I'm doing now?" or "I won't have to work with Harvey, will I? I really don't like him." Their relationship to the leader and the organization has been—and if they have their way, will continue to be—entirely transactional.

The leader's role in this shift is to paint a clear picture of where the organization is going and how each person can play a vital role in fulfilling the vision, but hard decisions almost inevitably need to be made. People who have been loyal workers but remain motivated only by the personal payoff need to be replaced with those who are intrinsically motivated by the new vision. The ones who no longer fit aren't necessarily malcontents—often they're friends who have worked hard but don't have the necessary skills for the new, bigger vision. They deserve respect, which makes these decisions even more difficult. The solution may be to move them *over* instead of *out*. We may be able to find another role in the organization for them, one where they fit better.

Some leaders simply can't have these painful conversations, so their team is like a racecar with a flat tire. They're trying to go fast, but they can't until the tire is replaced. Of course, in the process of this shift, we can't expect everybody on the team to get on board immediately. Some will, but others need time to consider what the change means for them. In this case, the tire with low pressure can be patched and the car can run fast. But after a reasonable period of time and a reasonable number of frank conversations, if a person on the team can't buy into the new direction, it's time to make a change.

In most cases, morale improves exponentially and is sustained for a long time when a person in the wrong role is moved to the right role or moved out. Good leadership requires making decisions that prioritize unity over the temporary comfort of avoiding hard conversations.

The shift from vision to unity taps into the intrinsic motivations of everyone on the team. They've already gone beyond basic agreement about expectations and have been moving at the speed of vision, working hard for a higher purpose. When they find they can be more effective with less effort at the speed of unity, the vast majority of them ask each other, "Where has this been all my life?" I've found that his shift happens much more easily and quickly than the other two. Of course, you may discover that someone insists on staying in the spotlight and doesn't want to share credit. That's where Christian leaders can point to Jesus, who came to serve, not to be served, and who always gave credit to the Father for every good thing. And it's where all of us can explain the concept of "servant leadership," the principle that guides the best leaders—like Jim Collins's Level 5 leaders—to be humble and yet have fierce resolve.

WHEN THEY FIND THEY CAN BE MORE EFFECTIVE WITH LESS EFFORT AT THE SPEED OF UNITY, THE VAST MAJORITY OF THEM ASK EACH OTHER, "WHERE HAS THIS BEEN ALL MY LIFE?"

THE LEADER'S SHIFT

The problem may not be whether the team members are willing to share the spotlight, but whether the leader is willing to share it. As leaders move into top gear, they have to change how they see their role.

The concept of servant leadership was first stated by Robert Greenleaf in a 1970 essay. He explained:

> The servant-leader is a servant first. . . . It begins with the natural feeling that one wants to serve, to serve first. Then conscious choice brings one to aspire to lead. That person is sharply different from one who is leader first, perhaps because of the need to assuage an unusual power drive or to acquire material possessions. For such it will be a later choice to serve—after leadership is established. The leader-first and the servant-first are two extreme types. Between them there are shadings and blends that are part of the infinite variety of human nature.

Greenleaf drew a contrast between traditional, top-down management and servant leadership, and he asked piercing questions that cause leaders to engage in serious self-evaluation:

> The difference manifests itself in the care taken by the servant-first leader to make sure that the other people's highest priority needs are being served. The best test, and difficult to administer, is: Do those served grow as persons? Do they, while being served, become healthier, wiser, freer, more autonomous, more likely themselves to become servants? And, what is the effect on the least privileged in society; will they benefit, or, at least, not be further deprived?[18]

The most common models of leadership are focused on the benefits to the leader—chiefly wealth, status, and power. But a servant leader, one who is relating to the team at the speed of unity, is focused on the benefits to the people around him and to those the team serves.

This leader delights in the success of others instead of being threatened by it. This way of leading is both global and specific: the leader makes a seismic shift in his leadership style and then makes hundreds of choices each day to live out this decision in connections with people on the team. Humility is demonstrated by the willingness to listen, empathy for people who are struggling, patience with those who aren't as quick to respond, and the joy in sharing credit for success. Their fierce resolve is demonstrated by their determination to bring out the best in people, to push them beyond their self-imposed limits, and to make the hard decisions that are inherent in leading any organization.

When a team is moving at the speed of unity, they experience a "rubber band effect." When the leader stretches them, they spring forward and sometimes go beyond the leader's ideas. When the team is functioning at this level, the leader isn't distracted by concerns about how the team will respond and what fires need to be put out. Instead, the leader can have "quicker courage" to make decisions and keep the team moving. They're drafting each other, and they're flapping in intricate unison. They still have disagreements, but these conversations sharpen them instead of dulling their effectiveness.

SWARMS, FLOCKS, AND HERDS

I love nature shows, and I'm fascinated by the behavior of large groups of fish, birds, and mammals like caribou. When we watch them, we notice that they move in exquisite unity. Most of the time, it's impossible to tell who is leading, but they're all coordinated, they defend the group from predators, and they look beautiful. Thousands, and sometimes tens of thousands, of animals move as one and seem to respond as a single unit to the current of the sea, the power of the wind, and the terrain where they run.

The shows often have scenes of predators who are looking for a member of the group that has strayed away, even for a few seconds. A pelican or shark picks off a straggling herring, a hawk dives on an unsuspecting and unprotected duck, and a wolf runs behind the herd, waiting for one to tire and fall back from the rest. When our teams are moving at the speed of unity, it's pretty obvious when someone strays. In many cases, others on the team don't wait for the leader to step in and challenge the person. They see that preserving the team's unity is everyone's responsibility, so they take action.

Adding new people is helpful to a team moving at the speed of agreement because the new hire brings skills to get a particular task done. Adding someone at the speed of vision requires more careful review of compatibility with the team's purpose. But for a team moving at the speed of unity, finding the right person is even more challenging because it assumes the person already has skills and drive; fitting into the culture is of primary importance—and the fit is, to some degree, subjective. These decisions must be made slowly, and often with the input of the most discerning people on the team, not just the leader or HR. They're looking for someone who already speaks the same language (or can pick it up very quickly), is willing to make sacrifices for the sake of the team, is glad to give credit to others, celebrates others' success, and already has a measure of the powerful blend of humility and resolve.

MY SHIFT TO THE SPEED OF UNITY

As I've mentioned, River Valley thrived on our clear vision, but after a few years, I intuitively sensed there was something missing . . . something more. As I talked to gifted leaders around the country, I heard a common theme in their explanation of how they shifted into top gear: at different points, they had to make the hard choices to replace people who couldn't or wouldn't move at their speed. This isn't a cruel choice. We're not fair or gracious when we expect people to do things they don't want to do or can't do. It's best for them and for our organizations to help them find a better fit.

Don't misunderstand: by this time at River Valley, everybody on the team had the same vision, and they were working hard to achieve it, but a few weren't in harmony with the rest. They were emotionally draining or they had become organizational outliers. When I made the change, we almost immediately started moving faster. This was an example of "addition by subtraction." When the people who weren't in harmony with us left, our team was more efficient and effective. We could move faster with less drag when the one out of alignment was gone.

The people we eliminate in the shift from chaos to agreement might be lazy, incompetent, passive, or vindictive; the people we let go in the shift from agreement to vision insist on a transactional relationship to the boss and the organization, and they don't care about having a greater impact; the people we fire in the shift from vision to unity are talented and dedicated, but they still want too much credit, they aren't supportive of others, and they drift away from the herd too often. They play a "zero-sum game": I win, you lose. They believe the pie is only so big, and they want a larger piece of it. These people have high competency but low chemistry. When a team is moving at the speed of agreement and vision, you can afford to keep people who are highly competent even if they're jerks. You pay a price to use their talents, but that's not a price you can afford at the speed of unity.

Today, the people who remain on our team are those who believe the universe of possibilities is constantly expanding, and it's a privilege to be part of a team that has limitless goals. They believe there's no end of the available resources and no limit on celebrations. As a nature junkie, I've learned that the universe is expanding faster than scientists dreamed only a few years ago.[19] That's a picture I have of River Valley—expanding our impact further and faster than any one of us (even me) dreamed only a short time ago, and it will continue to expand. I want people on our team who have that level of optimism, talent, and joy in working with each other. Nothing else and nothing less will do.

NO GOING BACK

When a leader and a team get a glimpse of the speed of unity, they can't settle for the lower gears any longer. It's like seeing great paintings by Rembrandt or Picasso, being inspired by them, and then seeing something I've tried to paint. It just doesn't do anything for you!

Walter Isaacson wrote a great book about Steve Jobs, and the book was turned into a movie, with Ashton Kutcher starring in the lead role. When I watched the film, I almost stood up and cheered in a scene when Jobs made the difficult executive decision I've been describing. Francis was the most gifted programmer at Apple, and he had been instrumental in the company's rise. But in the scene, Jobs determined was time for Francis to go:

Jobs: "Get . . . out! You're done."

Francis: "What? Are you gonna fire me?"

Jobs: "No! I ALREADY FIRED YOU! Why are you still here?"

Bill Atkinson tries to step in to change Jobs's mind: "Steve, he, he was our best programmer in the division."

Jobs: "He's the best programmer that doesn't care about our vision."

In the darkness of the theater, Becca grabbed my arm so I didn't make fool of myself. If she hadn't been there, I would have stood and yelled, "That's the speed of unity! High competency and low chemistry won't work! Drop the mic, Steve!"

But you don't necessarily have to fire people to get to the speed of unity. If you share the concept of the power of harmony—and they get it—the people already on the team can make the shift. I mentioned NBA coach Phil Jackson in the first chapter. The story of his greatness as a leader perfectly illustrates the point about bringing people along and helping them shift to top gear. Before he moved to Los Angeles to take over as the Lakers' coach in 1999, the team had All-Stars Shaquille O'Neal and Kobe Bryant, but they had flamed out in the early rounds of the playoffs too often. Jackson had won three championships as coach of the Chicago Bulls when he had Michael Jordan and Scottie Pippen. Could he work his magic in LA?

He could and he did. The Lakers were NBA champions in Jackson's first three seasons at the helm, and they won five titles in his dozen years. His critics complained that anybody could coach players like Jordan, Pippen, O'Neal, and Bryant to championships, but in fact, the only one of them to win a title without Jackson as their coach was O'Neal in Miami in 2006. Clearly, he brought something to the team that enabled the players' incredible talent to achieve ultimate success. He brought chemistry.

Jackson retired after the 2010-2011 season. After the last game that year, Kobe Bryant reflected on Jackson's leadership: "It's tough to put into words what he's meant to me. I grew up under him. The way I approach things, the way I think about things—not only in basketball but in life in general—a lot of it comes from him. It's a little weird for me to think about how next year's going to be."[20]

The speed of unity takes organizations where they could never go before. They may have been good, but now they're great. The may have experienced some success in the past, but nothing like this. Companies who shift into this gear create great products, teams win championships, and churches have an impact that's deep and wide. Each person experiences a level of fulfillment that stays with them for the rest of their lives. The leaders of these organizations multiply themselves in the lives of those they lead, and these people spread the idea wherever they go so other organizations learn to move at the speed of unity.

Whatever you do, don't miss this.

THINK ABOUT IT:

1. What are some ways shifting into the speed of unity would change (or already has changed) the effectiveness of your team?

2. Describe the challenges and benefits of shifting:
   ... from chaos to agreement:
   ... from agreement to vision:
   ... and from vision to unity:

3. What are the characteristics of servant leadership? Why is it essential for a leader who wants to move the team and the organization at the speed of unity?

4. Are you willing to make the hard decisions to let people go, even if they're highly competent, because they don't fit the chemistry you're trying to create? Have you proven that you're willing? Explain your answer.

5. What is the personal and organizational price for you to shift into the speed of unity? Are you willing to pay it? Why or why not?

CHAPTER 5

MAKE IT HAPPEN!

If you could get all the people in an organization rowing in the same direction, you could dominate any industry, in any market, against any competition, at any time.

PATRICK LENCIONI

After I spoke about the speed of vision at our church, a businessman approached me. I was talking with someone else, and out of the corner of my eye, I could tell he was about to pop! When the other person walked away, he almost jumped into my personal space and said, "Pastor Rob, I need every person in our company to hear this talk! I've got some work to do. I know that. We're between agreement and vision, but I want them to hear about the speed of unity so they'll know what's possible."

As the president of a biotech company, he understood that the principles I described go far beyond the church world. He is one of countless people who instantly understands what I'm talking about. They've had many of the same ideas, and they've read a lot of books about vision and organizational growth, but there's something about identifying the three speeds that makes a lot of the puzzle pieces suddenly fit in place. What he didn't say, but I'm sure he meant, was: "I sure wish I'd come up with this concept, but since you did, I'm going to send the link to this talk to everyone in my company." Before he walked away, he told me, "The speed of unity is going to be the new language of our company—for our purpose, our analysis, our planning, and our metrics."

I asked, "That's fantastic! Do you have what you need?"

He smiled, "Yeah I do, and I'm going to make it happen."

Let me be very practical about the steps leaders need to take to "make it happen" so they can move at the speed of unity.

CLARIFY YOUR VISION

If your organization or team is in chaos, there are other books you need to read and organizational consultants you need to hire to help you cut through the jungle of chaos to get to the speed of agreement.[21] For our purposes, I'm going to assume readers are at least at the speed of agreement. If you're at that speed, take time to think, pray, and talk until your vision is crystal clear. Then become a master at communicating it. Here's a good marker: After you've crafted it, written it, edited it, and then communicated it for a few weeks to your team, can they repeat it without reading it? If not, your vision isn't compelling enough, isn't simple enough, or isn't clear enough. Don't stop until it's so powerful that becomes the background music for everybody in the organization.

THE VISION NEEDS TO BECOME "THE LANGUAGE OF THE EMPIRE."

The vision needs to become "the language of the empire." People in different departments and teams in the business world will have their own language of production, sales, accounting, and marketing. In the church, different teams are responsible for music, children, young adults, senior adults, other target audiences, outreach, missions, care for the poor, and communications, and they have languages of their own. But across all these various teams, everyone needs to own the vision because it provides two necessities: focus and coherence. Everyone has the same ultimate purpose, and they're motivated to coordinate their efforts to reach their common goal.

The speed of vision is fast, but there's another gear. To move at the speed of unity, leaders need to align their teams with the vision, enlist the very best people to join them, and empower them to be successful. Let's look at these three necessities.

ALIGN

You can't align the people on your team if your vision isn't clear. With a vision, however, you can more easily see who fits and needs to be given more responsibility, who fits and is the right place already, who doesn't fit and needs to be reassigned, and who doesn't fit and needs to find a better situation somewhere else. The vision lets you articulate "Here's who we are," "Here's where we're going," and "Here's how we're going to get there." In the context of this explanation, you identify the values—for the team, relating to other teams in the organization, and how you treat customers or those who attend your church. If any of your people can't buy into all aspects of the vision and how you'll relate to each other, it's time for some candid conversations.

I like to think of this stage as weeding the garden. When he went on vacation, a friend of mine hired a high school kid in his neighborhood to cut his grass. Before he left, he told the young man, "If you see any weeds in the flowerbeds, please pull them up." When he got back two weeks later, about a third of his flowers and small bushes were gone, including some my friend had carefully dug up and replanted every time his family moved. Here's the point: the first job of a gardener is to know the difference between a weed and the plants he wants to keep.

One of the things I've noticed in my yard is that weeds often grow much faster than the flowers. That's a bummer. The corollary is that the impact of people who are weeds in our organizations can spread faster than the positive influence of the optimistic, diligent people. As I've pointed out, it's very tempting to keep high-performing people even if they have a very negative effect on us and our teams. We come up with all kinds of excuses to keep them, but their toxic impact spreads rapidly.

When I initially cast the vision for our church to be multi-site—one church in many locations—a couple of our staff members came to me and complained, "What is this about? Are you trying to take over the world?" Then one of them dropped the hammer: "Pastor Rob, Is this just an ego thing for you?" If they hadn't had a cynical scowl on their faces, I would have taken these as perfectly valid questions, ones I'd already asked myself and was ready to answer. Their questions weren't wrong, but their attitudes were. They weren't looking for clarity; they were accusing me of selfish motives. I wanted them to align with the vision, even if it took some time, but they weren't willing. Neither of them stayed with us very long after that day.

When I cast a vision and seek alignment, I want everybody to jump on the train. When they don't, I try to explain more fully, and I give them some time. Eventually, if they can't or won't get on board, I have to do what I dread doing: let them go. On the other hand, there have been times when I was sure staff members weren't going to align with a new vision, but actually, they were thrilled with it. It seemed that they had been waiting for the new vision all their lives! I learned the important lesson that I shouldn't prejudge responses.

Actually, clarity of purpose, transparency, and focus enable team members to regularly do self-assessments to see if they're still in alignment with the organization's vision. Quite often, those who aren't in alignment feel disconnected and uncomfortable, and many choose to move on. Those who remain are fiercely dedicated. In this way, clarity unifies the team. A muddled vision allows unmotivated people to stay too long, contributing little and often causing their fair share of headaches. Is it their fault? Yes and no. It's always important for people to dig deep and find their own sources of motivation, but leaders are responsible to create a vibrant environment and select the right people for the team.

First and foremost, alignment addresses attitude, but other factors include the person's experience, capacity, and talents. As the organization is moving faster, some wonderful people will have trouble keeping up. They're out of alignment, but we treat them very differently from those who oppose us. In churches and businesses, we may look down on people "who can't cut it" because they don't have exemplary skill sets, but that's totally inappropriate . . . and harmful to those people as well as the ones who are watching how we treat them.

When a tremendously talented high school pitcher is drafted by a major-league team, everyone expects the kid to win a Cy Young in a few years. When he hits his ceiling in Double-A ball and never makes it to the majors, we don't blame him for being inferior. We don't grumble, "What a loser!" Instead, we put our arm around him and say, "Way to go! You gave it everything you've got. I'm so proud of you!" The same dynamic is true in business and the church: some wonderful, dedicated people hit a ceiling—and it's not a character flaw. We need to find a really good place for them so they can continue to contribute and thrive—and we affirm them like crazy as they make the transition.

In sports—and especially, it seems, in professional basketball—one player can make a huge difference when he joins a team. He may have had difficulties in the system of his previous team, but when he fits in the chemistry of the new team, he excels. On smaller teams, like basketball or an executive team, the need for alignment is even more important than on larger teams. However, on smaller teams, moving someone is often more difficult.

One of the most important leadership traits for those who want to move at the speed of unity is the biblical concept of "dying to self." This is the humility of Level 5 leaders. We don't do only what's convenient for us or what will make people like us. We make the hard decisions, almost always decisions about people, so we'll have the right people who have the attitude, capacity, and skills to work together to fulfill the vision. In this environment, each person on the team also has to "die to self," recognizing the vision is more important than a position or a title. This requires humility and flexibility, a willingness to go anywhere and do anything for the greater good. This kind of humility is virtually non-existent in chaotic organizations, rare in those who are moving at the speed of agreement, more common for those with a compelling vision, and essential for teams that want to move at the speed of unity.

WE MAKE THE HARD DECISIONS, ALMOST ALWAYS DECISIONS ABOUT PEOPLE, SO WE'LL HAVE THE RIGHT PEOPLE WHO HAVE THE ATTITUDE, CAPACITY, AND SKILLS TO WORK TOGETHER TO FULFILL THE VISION.

Actually, it's harder to get alignment for a vision than for unity. The vision challenges people's concept of their purpose and their roles. If they make it through that stage, the ones who are on the team usually are already predisposed to value unity, but that's not always the case. I've had staff members who loved our vision but were toxic to the unity of the team. It's rare, but it happens. Far more often, the people who are excited about our vision are eager to do whatever it takes to achieve it. They're eager to shift into top gear. Those people are my delight!

In alignment, chemistry is crucial. One of the inherent problems of leadership is that we can be totally unaware of the damage caused by a toxic team member. In almost every organization that's trying to move faster, we'll find a key employee who appears to be in perfect alignment with the leader and the vision, but who's poisoning relationships with people in his sphere of influence. Quite often, when the leader meets with this person, the team member's reports and the interaction are all sweetness and light because that's what he wants the leader to hear. Only later, after a lot of damage has been done and offended people finally have the courage to speak up, the leader discovers what's really going on. At that moment, a leader's natural inclination is to wonder, *I can't be that wrong, can I?* And the obvious answer is, "Uh, yeah, you can."

A leader's commitment to alignment is like a parent with her kids. If she ignores bad behavior, the child's attitude will have a ripple effect throughout the family and result in problems for the rest of the child's life. Some parents are lazy and make mistaken assumptions like, "Ahh, it's not that bad," or "He'll grow out of it," or "It's no big deal. Everybody's doing it." But if organizations are going to get to the speed of unity, leaders can't afford to ignore passive or destructive attitudes and actions. If they wink at the bad behavior of high performers, cut side deals to keep them around, or avoid confronting real problems, they send a loud and clear message to everyone on the team that they really don't value unity at all. They show they love the person and the rest of the team by speaking the truth in love and giving the wayward team member an opportunity to change. In parenting and leadership, that's the goal: restoration, not condemnation.

ENLIST

Without alignment, it's impossible to enlist the best people. At one point I was slow to fire one of our team members who was causing friction but was a high performer. We interviewed a young man, I'll call him Darryl, to join our team. When I met with him, we hit it off, but when he met with the guy who was causing such friction, he immediately came to the conclusion there was no way he was going to work at River Valley. It didn't matter how big the vision was, Darryl knew he didn't want to work on a team that allowed a guy to create and inflame tension. Two years later, we had an opening on a different team. Someone suggested we contact Darryl, but I said, "I don't know about him. We gave him a shot, and it appears he doesn't love us." When I met with Darryl and heard his story, I realized why he had been hesitant before. He not only fits the role we outlined for him, he aligns with the overall vision, and from the beginning, he wanted to run at the speed of unity. And now, especially since the guy who was a problem is no longer in that leadership role, Darryl is cranking! In my first attempt to enlist Darryl, I was slow to see the threat to unity, but Darryl saw it immediately.

Caleb Brose is another example of a person who has been on the same page with us from the first day. When he came to us, I knew only some of his competencies, but I could see that the chemistry was terrific. He loves our vision and what we're doing! Since he's joined us, I've seen more of his amazing talents. We found a place for him because of his character and chemistry, and we've moved him to new positions because of his competence and capacity. I used to hire people strictly for their competence. No longer. The fact is that when you hire at the speed of vision, you're looking for people to get things done, but when you hire for unity, you're looking at who your team and your organization are going to become. Unity is far more than a job description. *Good* teams are full of talented performers, but *great* teams are full of talented performers who like each other, collaborate with each other, and push each other to excel.

At the speed of agreement, people are saying, "What do you want me to do, and what will I get out of it? I'll work for my salary and benefits." At the speed of vision, they're saying, "What do you want me to do? I want to play a part because it will open new opportunities for me. I'll work hard for you because I believe in what we're trying to accomplish." And at the speed of unity, they're saying, "I'm excited to serve together to do something great! I love the vision, I love the values, I love the people, and it's a privilege to contribute. I'm laying my life down for the team and the cause." That's what we've experienced on our team at River Valley. (One of our staff members told me, "Pastor Rob, I love this so much! You could shoot me, and I'd say, 'Thank you!'" I'm not sure everybody would describe the speed of unity this way, but I like it!)

I wish I could say that I'm the guru of discernment, but that wouldn't be the truth. A couple of years ago, we hired two people on the same day, and I introduced them to Becca. That night she told me, "This one fits and will do well, but that one isn't going to make it." In a single conversation with them, she could sense the presence or absence of chemistry.

In the shift from the speed of vision to the speed of unity, hire people with great talent, but more importantly, hire talented people who have great hearts.

EMPOWER

You may have noticed that I've used the word "love" a number of times. That may surprise you, especially if you work in a business context. I assure you, though, that I unapologetically, unequivocally assert that love is the fuel for teams to run at the speed of unity. In agreement people are motivated by fear and personal payoffs, and in vision they're motivated by accomplishing the goal, but in unity they're motivated by love and the fact that there's no ceiling on what might be accomplished.

I ASSURE YOU, THOUGH, THAT I UNAPOLOGETICALLY, UNEQUIVOCALLY ASSERT THAT LOVE IS THE FUEL FOR TEAMS TO RUN AT THE SPEED OF UNITY.

Some are reading this and saying, "Yeah, right. That may work in a church, but it doesn't work in business." But others want to shout, "I've never seen it in church either!" Fair enough. Let's take a hard look at this. It should come as no surprise for those who are familiar with the Bible that God's supreme value is love—sacrificial love, demonstrated by Jesus giving himself for us on the cross. The theme of love is woven throughout the pages of Scripture, and the writers warn us that anything less is a counterfeit of a true experience of God.

In one of his letters, the Apostle Paul tells the bickering, jealous people in the church in Corinth that there is no substitute for love: incredible spiritual power is only noise if it's not exercised with love, outstanding spiritual accomplishments mean nothing if they're not motivated by love, and personal generosity and dramatic sacrifice don't earn any points if love doesn't propel them (1 Corinthians 13:1-3). Love must be the beginning, middle, and end of how we relate to God and people.

So, how are you doing with that? What grade would you give the church in our country? Barely passing? A big fat F? Even if the broader church family has earned a checkered reputation, that's no excuse for giving up or turning to manipulation to get people to do what we want them to do. Love matters. I know someone genuinely loves me if they know the worst about me and love me still. When we're completely known and deeply loved, we don't have to wear masks to pretend we're someone else, and we don't have to spend our time worrying about what people think of us. We can relax, give and receive love, and have life-giving connections with people. No one does it perfectly, but even our flawed attempts are far better than intimidating, withdrawing, or sucking up to people to win their approval. A culture of love is the kind of environment some Christians have created over the centuries, and it's what God wants every church to build.

In the world of business, Jim Collins showed that leaders of the very best companies create environments of support, encouragement, and affirmation—we might call it love. In an article for *Forbes* titled, "The Biggest Motivator at Work? Love," Stefano Tasselli explains:

> As we know, organizations are obsessed with measurable performance and efficiency. But if managers want to motivate and keep their staff, they should appeal to their employees' passion and desire, which is impossible to quantify. My research has found that many organizations fail to recognize the obvious fact that an organization is made up entirely of people. And

> the truth is, people are motivated by love. . . . So, if you really want to retain and motivate your employees you have to look away from data driven reports and look at the relationships within your organization. Exploring the importance of love will uncover new opportunities and help us understand our organizations, our teams and ourselves.[22]

Today, the younger generation places a high value on relationships in the workplace. Many of them simply won't tolerate anything close to a stagnant or hostile environment. They're "quitting their boss" to find another one who values relationships as much as performance. In an article on a human resources website, Kristen Goodell tells bosses what they need to know about Millennials:

> Explore what motivates your millennials. Growing to their full potential and helping others do the same is so much more important than growing the company. Millennials want to work in a culture in which people matter and their talent is cultivated. They care about the employer's position on "giving back" to the community and deeply consider the employer's mission. They want to participate in an organization with a public purpose.
>
> Millennials are all about fairness and establishing boundaries. Workers will split if they feel they have a micromanager or absent boss. Many employees would rather switch companies than deal with a boss who will not let them complete a task without interfering, or with a boss that disappears and does not support their needs.[23]

Okay, great, but where does this level of love come from? The worst thing leaders can do is fake it. Their people can smell a rat from a distance, and the lack of authenticity will be another hurdle for the leader to jump over in building credibility with his people. We have to embody the love we want to express, and it can't be manufactured artificially. It must come from inside. We can love people—even those who annoy us and are, for some reason, seemingly unlovable—only to the extent that we feel completely known and deeply loved, that people know the worst about us and love us still. We can forgive people—especially those who have hurt us deeply and don't care what they've done—only to the extent that the well of our experience of forgiveness is full and overflowing. And we can accept people—especially people who have different ideas and values—only to the extent that we've been amazed that someone has accepted us when we were hard to accept. That's how God loves, forgives, and accepts us. (See 1 John 4:10-11, Ephesians 4:32, and Romans 15:7.)

The love we express for people in our organizations can't be a manipulative technique to get better results out of them. When you hear people talk about their jobs, they often describe their relationships, and especially, their relationship with their boss. And when you hear people speak at retirement parties, they don't bring out an Excel spreadsheet and point to production or sales numbers; they talk about how much people mean to them.

But let me be clear: I'm not advocating a sentimental love that has no backbone. Genuine love is invested in the good of the other person and is willing to say and do whatever is necessary to help that person succeed. If a person on the team is habitually late or failing in a responsibility, is it love to avoid the topic and act like everything is fine? Of course not. But it's not love to blast the person to smithereens, either. Love wades in, speaks the truth in a way the other person can understand, communicates affirmation and encouragement, and paints a picture of the future that inspires hope. And if there's no change, does love mean we just ignore it and shrug our shoulders? No way. We may try to restore the person another time or two, but when we're convinced no substantive change is coming, the most loving thing we can do is hold the person accountable and provide an appropriate exit.

COUNTERINTUITIVE

The process I've described of going from the speed of agreement to the speed of unity may seem upside down and backward. You might be thinking, *How can I fire my top performers and be more successful? It just doesn't make sense.* You're right, it doesn't make sense if you're only going to replace high performers with low chemistry with other high performers with low chemistry. But if you replace them with talented people who are on board with your culture, you'll be more successful, you'll reduce the strains on you and the rest of the team, you'll spend more time investing your creative energies in the mission, you'll enjoy your role as a leader, and you won't kick your dog every night when you go home.

When a person doesn't fit your chemistry, he emits a smog that pollutes, to some degree, everyone on the team. If you want to move at the speed of unity, you'll have to dig deep and find the courage to make some hard decisions. If you want better alignment, you have to realize when some people aren't aligned with you and your vision. And if you want unity, you need to create a culture that attracts, keeps, and launches people who are both high performance and high chemistry.

As these principles have become clearer to me, I've had more confidence making hard personnel decisions. Not long ago I had to make another one to let someone go. I told our team, "It was a difficult decision, but it was certain. For the good of the mission, I had to make it."

Implementing these principles puts us on a learning curve—no one does them well at the beginning. As you practice them, you'll find the courage to make the decisions you know you need to make. Humility and resolve . . . that's you.

THINK ABOUT IT:

1. As you read the section about alignment, who are the people out of alignment—perhaps with high competence but low chemistry—who came to mind? (No pointing, please!)

2. What's a good process to address this problem? Who needs to be affirmed, who needs to be moved to a better role, and who needs to find another church or company?

3. As you think about hiring people who are consistent with your chemistry, what are you (or will you be) looking for?

4. Who are the people who have loved you, supported you, and believed in you? What difference have they made in your life? How are you letting those experiences shape how you treat people on your team?

5. This chapter has a lot of directions and suggestions. What are your top three priorities as you take steps to move toward the speed of unity?

CHAPTER 6

GET PEOPLE ON BOARD

You don't get unity by ignoring the questions that have to be faced.

JAY WEATHERILL

When some people read the last chapter, they were ready to jump out of their seats. They're saying, "Yes! That's what I want! If our team can move at the speed of unity, it'll be fantastic . . . but can it really happen?"

Yes, I assure you it can. In fact, I'm convinced it's the future of business, the church, and nonprofit organizations. But other people have read this far, and they're not having happy thoughts about me. Some want to yell, "You told my leader to fire me! And in fact, I think you offered to help him get rid of me! Thanks a lot." And others are scratching their heads and wondering, "It all sounds really good, but I'm pretty sure my leader isn't buying the need to move at the speed of unity. I'm not the president, CEO, or pastor. How can I do this from my position in the organization?"

At each speed, leaders are looking for different things from their team members. At the speed of agreement, they expect their people to perform the assigned tasks, to live up to the job description, and to avoid making waves. At the speed of vision, leaders take the transactions at the speed of agreement for granted, and they go further: they expect their people to share a common goal and work together to achieve it. At the speed of unity, both of the traits and expectations of the first two gears are baked in, and now, the leader expects the team to have a higher level of trust, vulnerability, creativity, and mutual encouragement.

I've noticed that when teams are in the first gear, the team members' questions often have an edge to them. They're trying to pin the leader down . . . and maybe make him look foolish: "Why are we doing that?" "Do you really think that'll work?" "Who thought that was a good idea?" Of course, not all questions are like that, but it only takes a few to make everybody defensive. To change the metaphor, these teams are about as coordinated as a first-grade band recital!

In the second gear, questions are meant to clarify goals and processes, and the underlying motive is for the person asking the question to be sure he or she is getting the job done and receiving credit. These teams are like a rock band—lots of movement and often loud . . . and very entertaining!

But at the top speed, when people feel more comfortable with each other and more supportive of each other, questions aren't subtle attacks; they're ways to connect on a deeper level, to maintain unity and deepen it as people interact to make sure everyone is on the same page. These teams function like a professional symphony playing Beethoven or Mozart, in beautiful synchrony, with each person having a vital role.

THESE TEAMS FUNCTION LIKE A PROFESSIONAL SYMPHONY PLAYING BEETHOVEN OR MOZART, IN BEAUTIFUL SYNCHRONY, WITH EACH PERSON HAVING A VITAL ROLE.

In an orchestra, the conductor and the musicians spend a lot of time in practice so they know each other very well. The conductor hears the quality of each person's instrument and gives input to help them pursue excellence and harmonize with the others. And the musicians become students of the conductor's passions and preferences so they can adjust to make the symphony as beautiful and powerful as it can be. The intricacy, beauty, and power of an orchestra is a model of what happens on teams that are learning to move at the speed of unity.

LEADER, KNOW YOUR TEAM

Leaders have risen to their place of responsibility because, in most cases, they've been gifted and assertive. They've been one of the smartest people in the room, and their leadership is based on superior knowledge and skills. Although those are positive traits, they can be severe hindrances to team chemistry. In an article for *Inc.,* Thomas Koulopoulos, the founder of Delphi Group, observes that leaders often are so intent on giving directions that they don't listen well. But he goes further: Listening is the first step, but . . .

> . . . listening alone isn't enough. To be a great leader, who inspires trust in others, you need to demonstrate that you not only hear them but that you "get them." . . . A leader is only a leader because people choose to follow him or her. And getting people to follow you is about having them believe that you understand them, not that you're smarter than them. Humans are extraordinary complex creatures. We long for understanding, and we instantly sniff out when someone is trying to understand or just being patronizing. Your job as a leader is to really hear what people are saying, not what you want to hear or what you think you heard.[24]

To go beyond transactional relationships with the people on their teams, leaders need to build trust. People in HR can identify many different tips and techniques for trust building. Let me offer just a few:

Practice reflective listening.

When someone tells you something, you can respond by saying, "This is what I hear you saying . . ." and put it in your own words. If you got it right, both of you feel understood. And if you got it wrong, the person can say, "Not quite. Here's what I meant . . ." Either way, you've made a better connection.

Major on the majors.

The intensity of your emotions broadcasts what's important to you. If you're passionate about everything, the people on your team will be confused . . . and they'll be exhausted. Sometimes, when something doesn't go as planned, you don't need to do a detailed analysis and assign blame; you just need to smile and shrug and move on. Some things are exceptionally important, others are fairly important, and still others aren't that important at all. Know the difference.

Value input.

First, ask for others' input, and then, let your team members know it's important to you by valuing what they have to say. Quite often, someone who has been quiet will voice an idea that proves to be the answer to a sticky problem. Even if you don't follow through with every suggestion, the affirmation of a person's contribution builds confidence and trust.

Be a spotlight.

Be relentlessly positive about your people—not phony, but sincere and specific. If you don't affirm them and their work, they'll wonder if they belong on the team at all. But blanket statements like, "You're great!" don't have the impact of a specific affirmation like, "Beth, when you took extra time with that client, she really appreciated it. Your obvious care and your explanation made all the difference. Thank you."

Model empathy.

There's probably no leadership trait that contributes to unity more than the ability to deeply understand and connect emotionally with the people on the team. When they believe we see their hearts and we care about them, petty grievances seem to evaporate, and significant problems find solutions. Many of us are tempted to use our position of power to command. This strokes our egos and puts people "in their rightful place" beneath us, but leaders who insist on dominating their teams will only achieve compliance (at best) at the speed of agreement.

We may come up with a dozen excuses why this approach doesn't fit our leadership style, our company's goals, or the culture of our team. Those excuses are valid, however, only if you want to stay at the speed of agreement or vision. The speed of unity requires us to acquire these traits and sharpen our skills. You're asking a lot from your team to move at top speed, and now you need to ask a lot of yourself. But don't worry. It's worth it.

Leaders need to create "inside-outside" connections for the team. Relationships that exist only inside the walls of the organization during business hours will only go so far. That's where the job gets done, but it's not the only place where relationships are developed. The speed of unity can only be achieved when leaders and their teams take the titles off their shirts and become equals outside the office. When people on a team tell me they're playing together in a golf league, or they're going to the beach, or they're having dinner or a birthday party at someone's house, or any of a hundred other things friends do with each other, I can tell they're either already moving at the speed of unity or they're getting there.

THE SPEED OF UNITY CAN ONLY BE ACHIEVED WHEN LEADERS AND THEIR TEAMS TAKE THE TITLES OFF THEIR SHIRTS AND BECOME EQUALS OUTSIDE THE OFFICE.

Leaders who want to create bonding experiences carve out a day or two away from the office for the team to participate in a ropes course or hear each other's stories. These investments of time and money create the chemistry that pays huge dividends. The team gets to see the leader in a vulnerable situation on the obstacle course, and they get to hear the background story of the pain and joys that motivate him or her. Some people complain that these experiences are a waste of time, but if your leader plans them, go . . . and go with high hopes of deeper connections.

Inside and outside, in the office and away, take every opportunity to get below the surface and build stronger relationships.

TEAM MEMBER, KNOW YOUR LEADER

In agreement, team members know what's expected of them (hopefully), but they may not understand the organization's overall goals and strategy, and they almost certainly haven't grasped the leader's heart. They see themselves as cogs in the machine. In second gear, people on the team are captured by the vision, and they realize they play important roles in fulfilling it. They're motivated to make a difference, and they begin to get a glimpse of the leader's heart. If the team is going to move at the speed of unity, the leader has to be secure enough to drop his mask, lower his guard, admit his weaknesses, and reveal his hopes and fears. In fact, I think it's impossible to get to the speed of unity unless the people on the team know their leader's heart so that their respect and trust accelerate.

To help our staff at River Valley understand me better, I've developed a "user's manual" for them. Here's my thinking: If people need a manual like this for every piece of equipment they buy, they can use one to know how to relate to me. I didn't write this because I demand they treat me a certain way, but because I want them to know what matters to me and what they can do to make our relationship richer and deeper. I'll put the user's manual at the end of the chapter, but before we get there, I want to describe three commitments for everybody on the team: speak the language, sing the song, and wear the uniform.

Speak the language

When team members use the leader's words and phrases, they have a shared language, which builds unity. The leader has described the organization's values, vision, and strategy, and it greatly encourages him when he hears people on the team repeating things he has said.

If you're on a team, you probably have no idea how much it means to your leader to hear you quote him. When I hear someone talking to another staff member and say, "That's what it means to move at the speed of unity," I get really excited!

Sing the song

When we sing, two functions reinforce each other. Our minds focus on the words and the melody we're vocalizing, but we're also hearing ourselves in two ways, through the air and through the bones in the skull, a process called "bone conduction."[25] Singing produces greater commitment. Soldiers in training often sing in unison. Their song may be redundant and silly, but they're forming a deeper bond as they sing together. In the same way, when people on a team "sing" the vision together, they're reinforcing their own commitment to it, and they're building stronger connections with each other.

A big part of singing the song together is being tenaciously optimistic. At our church, one of our values is to "speak life." It's easy to get wrapped up in problems and dwell on the dark side of things. I'm certainly not suggesting we should deny reality; I'm advocating that even in the most difficult moments, we find sources of hope, love, and gratitude. We may speak the hard truth, but always while also speaking life.

When teams aren't singing in unison, it sounds like the needle is scratching across the record. Sarcasm, ridicule, and blame fill the air. You can't reach the top speed of unity when the team's music is cacophony.

When you have a transactional job, you put in only what you've agreed to contribute . . . no more. But when you create music, you put everything you are into it. You're more creative, more attentive, more passionate, and more interested in the outcome. Building a unified team is like crafting a beautiful song.

BUT WHEN YOU CREATE MUSIC, YOU PUT EVERYTHING YOU ARE INTO IT. YOU'RE MORE CREATIVE, MORE ATTENTIVE, MORE PASSIONATE, AND MORE INTERESTED IN THE OUTCOME.

Wear the uniform

When Olympic athletes walk into the stadium during the opening ceremony, everyone wears the same uniform. They may be famous celebrities whose names are known around the world, or they may be the most obscure person in a lesser-known sport. (Curling, anyone? As a side note, I have curled with the USA Olympic Gold medalists! Not many people can say that!) It doesn't matter—they're on the same team. On the last night when they come back for the closing ceremony, they wear the same uniform again. During the two weeks or so in between, they've worn the uniform of their particular sport, but always with their nation's colors. At every moment, they know they're representing much more than their individual talents—they're representing the hopes and dreams of everyone in the country.

When we're moving at the speed of unity, we're all wearing the same uniform of selfless commitment. We have our eyes on a goal that's much bigger and better than individual achievement, and we want the world to see *us,* not just *me.*

ESSENTIAL SUPPORT

I'm afraid some people will read what I've written in this chapter and conclude that I'm suggesting the speed of unity means everyone always has the same opinions. That's certainly not the case. For any team in any organization, there will be disagreements. Some of these can be resolved by compromise and finding a way to make everybody happy, but some can't. On our team, I invite people to voice their opinions and objections, but when the decision is made, I expect them to support the decision in their interactions with others on the team and those outside. I've seen too much damage from people grumbling that the leader didn't follow their suggestion. They privately complained to other people on the team, creating pockets of dissention, and they've complained to people outside, creating a wave of doubt about the leader's motives and good sense.

As our team moved into the speed of unity, I told them, "I want your input, but the buck stops with me. I'm sure you'll disagree with some of the decisions I make. I hope that most of the time you'll agree with our decisions and support them, but I guarantee there will be times when you don't feel good about one. The test of unity is how you communicate your displeasure. If you want to talk to me about it, I assure you that my door is open. If you and I have had an honest conversation, I hope you'll feel heard even if I don't agree with your point of view. When you walk out the door, you need to support the decision. I'm not talking about 'foot-dragging support'; I'm talking about *enthusiastic* support. You may not be enthusiastic about this particular decision, but I hope you can be supportive of the process, the team, and me. Let me be clear: I'm not insisting that you agree with me, but I insist that you support the decisions of the team. If you can't do that, especially if you feel like you need to go on a crusade to challenge my authority, it's time for you to find another place to work."

All of us who are leaders have seen people on our teams disagree with a decision, and they're tempted to have a bad attitude, like the jilted girlfriend at the wedding, to gossip and spread rumors, to withdraw, to feel sorry for themselves, or to be passive-aggressive and sabotage the team while insisting they did nothing of the sort. This person has become a dirt road detour to the team's speed of unity . . . and if the leader doesn't do anything about it, the leader takes his own detour.

MAYBE YOU

Many younger people are idealists who believe they can't support a leader unless they're 100 percent in agreement. This never turns out well. It's unrealistic to conclude you're going to agree all the time with a leader . . . or a spouse or friend or the mailman or anyone else. If that's you, keep your idealism and enthusiasm, but realize that making a significant contribution on a great team requires at least some compromise.

You may be a leader who doesn't feel confident that you can create a culture that moves at top speed. Don't despair, and don't give up. Go back to the previous chapter, read it again, swallow hard, and do what it takes to align the people on your team, enlist the right people, and empower them with love and courage.

Or you may be on a team that's stuck in reverse or at the speed of agreement. Is your situation hopeless? Do you need to work on your résumé? Maybe, but you might first try to find at least one person who is willing to create a micro-climate of encouragement. As the two of you enjoy your work and support each other, a few others might decide to join you. If your boss sees that you're more productive and you're a breath of fresh air in the office, maybe, just maybe, you can loan him this book and see what happens. If you're giving your best, supporting your boss, working with enthusiasm, and encouraging others on the team, yet your team doesn't change after six months or so, it's time to think about other options. Actually, you can be sure that leaders of other teams will notice and recruit you. You're much too valuable to stay stuck in a dead-end situation.

THE USER'S MANUAL

As promised, I want to include the material we give to everyone who joins our staff at River Valley. I want them to know me, understand me, and see into my heart. This tool has been invaluable for our team. Obviously, this is about me, my thoughts, my limits, and my motivations. You'll need to create your own that reflects your personality and preferences.

STAFF USER'S MANUAL

For the staff of River Valley Church to relate effectively to Pastor Rob Ketterling, know this:

THIS IS HOW I THINK.

- Everything is possible. I'm optimistic. I think the best is yet to come.
- My mind is always thinking about all different sorts of things and in all different sorts of directions.
- I think multitask, multifaceted, and multiple angles. I realize more is involved than what I see.
- I love to think in the way of "Possibility – Why not? – Perhaps God – Let's do it!"

- Stop making excuses, and let's make something happen!
- I think ahead. I have to be ahead of the team because I'm the leader.
- I think in segments: right now, today, this week, this month, this year, next ten years.

THIS IS HOW I LIKE THINGS DONE.

- I like things done on time, with excellence, and with an added twist. I like things done with an extra added value and intentionality.

HOW DO YOU GIVE NEW IDEAS WITHOUT KNOCKING DOWN PREVIOUS IDEAS?

- Use two words, "What if?"
- If you say, "I'm not sure this is the best way to do it," that leads to defensiveness.
- Bring me several possibilities. Are there more possibilities to the way we are doing something? Expand our thinking!
- Also use the words, "How about . . .?"
- Let's open it up and make it better, not knock what was.
- I believe that having lots of possibilities means we're all trying to make it better.
- When you bring an idea to the people, you need to show the problem first so they know we need a solution.
- When you bring an idea to the me, you need to show me the possibilities first.

HOW DO YOU PROMOTE PEOPLE?

- I promote people . . .

  . . . when I get a full feedback loop.

  . . . when I observe them doing well, their leaders say they are doing well, their peers say they are doing well, and their followers say they are doing well.

  . . . when I recognize a gifting with the right time and an opportunity.

  . . . when all these factors come together quickly, we can expedite the promotion.

- Some people think they can only kiss up to the leader, but you can't only kiss up to your leaders and get a promotion.

- Some people are promoted by faithfulness, and a position opening up can give them an opportunity.

HOW DO YOU MEASURE AND DEFINE SUCCESS?

- I measure success by results. But I have to be careful that this doesn't cause me to overlook character deficiencies. I have sometimes overlooked character deficiencies in skilled, effective people. In the long term, I need to see results paired with wholeness.

- I measure success by the number of people you are taking on the journey. If you churn through staff and volunteers, that's a real concern for me. Show me you had time for margin in your life because of all the people who are helping you.

- I measure success in longevity—not just that you survived, but that you were thriving in your tenure.

- I measure success by people doing what they were supposed to do.

- Success is in the "yes!" Did you say "yes" and fulfill the "yes"?
- Success is not in the number, but in the "yes."
- Success is the pipeline of leaders under you.
- I want you to stay for four years. I hope you will stay ten, and I would love it if you stayed a lifetime.

PEOPLE I PAY ATTENTION TO:

- Whoever is helping us carry the load. I'm not going to pay attention to you if you aren't going to help us carry the load. You can carry it financially, through leadership, or through service.
- I want to give attention to the people who are lifting this load!
- If I have a free night, I want to give it to the people who are leading and lifting.

WHAT'S IMPORTANT TO YOU?

- Honesty and loyalty—every leader wants loyalty. You can ask questions, but judge your spirit before asking. Ask in a right spirit.
- There is no such thing as a "throwaway line." Anything you say is coming from somewhere in your heart.
- I don't like surprises. If there's information I need (Big Info), I would rather know now than be surprised by finding out later.

HOW TO RELATE TO MY FAMILY?

- I told the church early on, "You can forget my birthday, but don't forget my wife Becca's birthday!" I answered the call of God to plant this church. If anyone disrespects my family, it catches my attention and my defenses come up.

- I want people to honor my family, but I wouldn't like it to be flattery and appeasement. I look for authentic honor.
- Whenever you are talking about my family, you can't "unsay" what you said—so be careful!
- I pray that I would never be the one to wink at sin in my family like Eli did with his boys, Hophni and Phineas.
- If you are bringing me an issue about my family, keep it as closed a circle as possible. Let's try to deal with this and not spread gossip and misinformation.
- Honor Becca for her sacrifice.

HOW WOULD YOU WANT SOMEONE ON STAFF TO TELL YOU THEY WANT TO START A CHURCH?

- We are in an environment where we don't want to be the last church planted. We believe there's always room for more!
- Start with this: "I'm under your authority, and I'm thinking about starting a church."
- Next, I'll look at the clock: How long has the person been here, etc.?
- Next, I'll look at the runway: How long until takeoff?
- Keep the plans in tight circle of your family and closest friends. If tons of people know about it, you will unravel the plan too much and you limit the options.
- I want to be in on the process early, and I want to know the most flexible start date possible.

Here are some guidelines:

- Don't do anything that confuses the body of Christ.

- Try to protect the unity of this church and the churches in the area where you want to plant.
- Honor the other churches in your area.

HOW WOULD YOU WANT SOMEONE TELL YOU IF THEY WANTED TO LEAVE?

- We aren't going to keep everyone forever. We expect a minimum of four years, we hope for ten, and we're happy with a lifetime.
- In the same way people trusted us to hire them, we hope they will trust us to help them know when it's time to leave.
- Not everyone will stay forever, but everyone can leave well.

HOW IMPORTANT IS IT FOR YOU TO KNOW WHERE WE SEE OURSELVES IN 5 YEARS?

- A lot of churches don't like to know what people want to do in their future, but I love it!
- I want to know what's in your heart. Don't lie to us about plans to leave this place. Be honest and tell the truth.
- I'm mature enough to know that plans change, and God can adjust your trajectory.
- Use verbiage like, "I feel God is leading me there."
- Ask me how the team can make you ready for the next move, because getting ready may take 2 to 5 years

HOW WOULD YOU WANT SOMEONE TO SHARE A CHALLENGE WITH YOU?

- I want them to sidebar with me if they want to share a personal challenge with me or challenge something I'm doing at River Valley Church.
- The biggest thing a leader is thinking during a challenge is: "How big is the circle?" Is this person sharing a concern, or is he or she being disloyal?
- You want to show your loyalty by saying and meaning: "I love this enough to challenge it!"
- It's fighting words if you say, "A lot of people have been talking . . ." I'll want to know who so we can root out the enemy! So don't use this phrase.
- When challenging me, this is good verbiage, "This is on my heart. I don't know the whole picture, and I don't understand. Please help me."
- Always go to the person you report to unless you've gone to that person enough times with little or no results. Then it's appropriate to go to the next person up the chain of authority. The person over you can't help if you skip over him or her.

Important principles of engagement:
Agree – Support – Align

- When we leave the room after a decision is made, we need everyone to support the decision. —You don't have to agree with the decision. You can think, "I didn't agree with it, but I support it." It's disloyal to walk out of the meeting and tell people, "I don't like the decision." That breaks a team down.
- Agreement is the hope. Support is the necessity.

- Don't sabotage. You can sabotage a decision and a leader by a lack of enthusiasm, by letting people know you voted against a decision, or by not giving your full effort.

HOW SHOULD YOU RESPOND WHEN YOU MAKE MISTAKES?

- Admit it when you make mistakes. I don't expect you to be perfect, but I expect you to be aware and honest.
- When you make a mistake, don't give such a brief apology that people can't even feel your regret.
- Tell me all the things you're ready to do to resolve it! You can help your recovery by thinking of your own solutions!
- Allow time for your team to feel the hurt of the mistake.

  Admit you are wrong.

  Let it land.

  Move on.

- Take the same approach with your team in how you handle their mistakes.

HOW I COMMUNICATE:

Emails

- Bullet points and answers requiring a short response from me.

Texts

- These aren't intrusive at all. I actually like this best because it's brief, it's immediate, and then it's done.

Phone Calls

- Call if it's fun or you have an emergency.

In Person

- I need your nonverbals to match your words. I can read your nonverbal messages better than you realize!

HOW DO I GET MORE TIME WITH YOU?

- You need to get in my flight plan! Go where I'm going. Be proactive and be positive! Every leader wants to spend time with their team, but sometimes time constraints won't allow it.

MISCELLANEOUS THOUGHTS

- Golf is my favorite hobby.
- My wife jokes that I'm the "yes man." I usually say "yes" to anything, and those things tend to become sermon illustrations!
- My love language is words of affirmation.
- I hate to eat alone.
- I love to travel.
- I believe in giving people second chances!

THINK ABOUT IT:

1. If you're a leader, what are some specific principles you want to implement from the section about leaders? What's the first thing you'll do?

2. And if you're on a team, what does it mean for you to speak the language, sing the song, and wear the uniform?

3. How much effort does your team put into building deeper relationships? What can you do better? What difference will it make?

4. Is it authoritarian to expect people on the team to support the decisions? Explain your answer.

5. How would writing a "user's manual" help the people who join your team (and those who are already on it)?

CHAPTER 7

BIG TOWER, WRONG GOALS

The right thing, with the wrong motive, is the wrong thing.

BOB GOFF

The speed of unity is an incredibly powerful force, but it can be used for good or evil. To be honest, for me, it's almost inconceivable to believe that a person reading this book might use the power of the speed of unity for sinister purposes. I've seen it used in amazing ways for good, and that's what I want to focus on in this book, but it's necessary to take a hard look at ourselves to make sure we're not going full speed in the wrong direction.

Ancient and modern history show us the dark side of unity. In fact, one of the first recorded stories in all of literature is about people using the power of unity for wrong reasons. You may or may not be familiar with a story in the opening pages of the Bible about a time when people were unified in their passion for their own prestige and glory. With amazing unity, they came together to build the Tower of Babel.

THE TOWER

The writer of Genesis paints a picture of the power of unity for selfish goals. "At one time all the people of the world spoke the same language and used the same words." People came together, formulated a goal, crafted a strategy, and marshaled their resources to accomplish it. Then they said, "Come, let's build a great city for ourselves with a tower that reaches into the sky. This will make us famous and keep us from being scattered all over the world" (Genesis 11:1, 4). Scholars and archeologists tell us that the city of Babylon was built on this site, which is on the Euphrates River about sixty miles southwest of Baghdad in Iraq.

The people had a huge vision. They planned to build a stepped tower, called a ziggurat, that reached to the sky. It would be so impressive that they could always point to it and say, "Yeah, we did that! We're awesome." The tower was a monument to their talents, their planning, and their ambition . . . all totally apart from God and against God's instruction for people to spread out and fill the earth.

The Lord saw what the power of unity was accomplishing, and He said, "Look! The people are united, and they all speak the same language. After this, nothing they set out to do will be impossible for them! Come, let's go down and confuse the people with different languages. Then they won't be able to understand each other" (Genesis 11:6-7). Did you catch that? Because they were moving at the speed of unity, God knew that "nothing they set out to do will be impossible for them."

God stopped the construction of the tower by causing them to speak in many different languages. They couldn't understand each other, so they couldn't remain united in their vision and work.

The word *babel* means "to confuse, to mix, to mingle." That's why we say people are "babbling" when we can't understand them. The Bible's writers come back to the city of Babylon many times throughout the story of redemption, especially when the Babylonians conquered God's people in Judah and carried captives back to their city. Later, when John describes the end times in Revelation, Babylon represents all nations in rebellion against God and His people. The rebels have enormous power for evil, but in the end, they'll get what's coming to them.

In Genesis, the people were building an impressive tower, but their motive was entirely self-serving. They were moving at the speed of unity, but in the wrong direction!

THE FÜHRER

A more recent example of the speed of unity being used for evil is the history of Nazi Germany. Adolf Hitler had been an undistinguished corporal in World War I and, after the war, tried his hand at a number of jobs. He and a group of friends were angry about the way Germany had been treated in the Treaty of Versailles, and they planned a coup. It failed miserably. Hitler was arrested, convicted of sedition, and put in prison. While he was there, he wrote his manifesto, *Mein Kampf* ("my struggle"), describing his plans to take over the country, conquer Europe, and get rid of the Jewish population.

Years later, his small Nazi Party began to make inroads in German politics. They used ruthless tactics—beatings, kidnappings, and murder—to eliminate opposition and intimidate anyone who might resist them. Hitler rose to power as the German Chancellor at almost the same time Franklin Roosevelt became President of the United States, but the two men had very different visions for their countries.

During the 30s, Hitler consolidated power and changed his title to Führer: the supreme, unquestioned leader of the German nation. Germany had suffered terribly under the terms of the Versailles Treaty, and the people had spiraled into despair even as their economy collapsed around them. Hitler restored their honor and dignity by withdrawing from the treaty, building up the military, and using accounting sleight of hand to make it seem that the economy was roaring at the time the rest of the world struggled during the ravages of the Great Depression.

The German people loved Hitler, and they would follow him anywhere, even to death in war. The cult of personality in Germany during those years was rivaled by few other historic leaders, such as the Roman emperors and the Khans of Mongolia and China. Every soldier and sailor in Germany swore allegiance, but not to the nation. They swore a solemn oath of loyalty to one man: Adolf Hitler.

ALMOST TO A PERSON, THE PEOPLE OF GERMANY SPOKE THE NAZI LANGUAGE, SANG THE NAZI SONGS, AND WORE NAZI UNIFORMS (OR AT LEAST RIBBONS AND PINS). THEY WERE ALL IN.

The sea of uniforms at the annual Nuremburg rallies during the 30s and the pageantry of the 1936 Berlin Olympics were focused on the glory of one man. It certainly appeared that nothing was impossible for the nation under Hitler's leadership. Even as early as 1933, more than ninety percent of the Germans were "believers in the Führer." As dissent was quashed by arrests, concentration camps, and executions, the media was flooded with propaganda about Hitler's glories. An article in the German news media, *Spiegel,* explains that Hitler's "personal achievements" were constantly in front of the German people: "The personalized focus of the regime's 'successes' reflected the ceaseless efforts of propaganda, which had been consciously directed to creating and building up the 'heroic' image of Hitler as a towering genius, to the extent that Joseph Goebbels could in 1941 with some justification claim the creation of the Führer Myth to have been his greatest propaganda achievement."[26] Almost to a person, the people of Germany spoke the Nazi language, sang the Nazi songs, and wore Nazi uniforms (or at least ribbons and pins). They were all in.

Adolf Hitler and his Nazi associates created perhaps the most unified nation in history, and it was centered on a man who was at the time considered the savior of the nation, but now is seen for what he was: a diabolical megalomaniac. By 1939, the cult of personality was complete. In a speech in the Reichstag, the German congress, in April of that year, Hitler told the adoring crowd:

> I overcame chaos in Germany, restored order, enormously raised production in all fields of our national economy . . . I succeeded in completely resettling in useful production those 7 million unemployed who so touched our hearts . . . I have not only politically united the German nation but also rearmed it militarily, and I have further tried to liquidate that Treaty sheet by sheet whose 448 Articles contain the vilest rape that nations and human beings have ever been expected to submit to. I have restored to the Reich the provinces grabbed from us in 1919; I have led millions of deeply unhappy Germans, who have been snatched away from us, back into the Fatherland; I have restored the thousand-year-old historical unity of German living space; and I have attempted to accomplish all that without shedding blood and without inflicting the sufferings of war on my people or any other. I have accomplished all this, as one who 21 years ago was still an unknown worker and soldier of my people, by my own efforts . . .

Some people have been criticized for saying that Hitler was a great leader. I may be sawing off the limb I'm sitting on, but I think he was one of the most effective leaders I've ever read about. He galvanized a demoralized nation, restored their pride, and gave them a new sense of destiny—all for an evil purpose. He was great in his talents, but his motives were diabolical, and his impact was enormously destructive.

Hitler led his country and the world into a war that took the lives of fifty million soldiers and civilians and devastated many nations. The evil of Germany's unity was most clearly seen in the thirteen million people, including six million Jews, who were exterminated in the death camps. The speed of unity has probably never had such cataclysmic results. Thankfully, the Allies worked together to stop Germany and Japan from becoming dominant powers for evil in the world. It took time for the Allied powers to get up to speed, but they devoted virtually all of their financial resources, manpower, and industrial production to the single goal of defeating the cancer of the Nazis in Germany and the cruel militarism of Japan. In the United States, food was rationed, auto manufacturing was converted to produce tanks and airplanes, kids collected scrap metal, our young men marched off to fight, and the entire American culture became unified to rid the world of fascism.

RIGHT GOALS

All of us, in business and the church, are tempted to use our talents for selfish ends. The best of us fight hard against that natural human tendency and rivet our hearts on higher purposes: to make products and provide services to make our customers' lives better, and to help people to become fully devoted followers of Jesus. In both of these, our talents are means to noble ends. Let me use a couple of examples from Scripture and church history to illustrate the point.

Jesus had been with His disciples for over three years. They had watched Him heal the sick, cleanse lepers, give sight to the blind, and raise the dead. They had seen the religious leaders try to tear Him apart with verbal assaults . . . and then conspire with the Romans to literally tear Him apart on the cross. They were devastated by the death of Jesus but were amazed three days later when He came out of the grave! Over the next forty days, He met with them, reassured them, and taught them. He was preparing them for new responsibilities in the greatest enterprise the world has ever known, and none of them could do it alone. Ten days after Jesus ascended back to heaven, His followers were in Jerusalem, waiting as He had instructed for a fresh surge of power. Over a hundred people were in a room, anticipating . . . hoping . . . expecting something wonderful to happen. Luke tells us, "Now when the day of Pentecost had come, they were all with one accord in one place" (Acts 2:1 WEB). The Holy Spirit came and empowered them to fulfill Jesus' purpose of beginning to take the gospel of grace to everyone in the world. They couldn't do it unless they were "all with one accord."

Then, a century or two later, the early church demonstrated the power of moving at the speed of unity. Granted, the history of the church is checkered. At times, the church has become self-absorbed and petty. We've been more concerned about our comfort and honor than being Jesus' voice, hands, and feet to care for others. We haven't even moved at the speed of agreement—we've raced backwards! Yet followers of Jesus were agents of healing during two devastating plagues in the second and third centuries, after unbelievers evacuated and left infected family members to die. The first outbreak, about 165 a.d., was probably smallpox. The second, starting in 251 a.d., may have been measles. In each case, about a fourth of the people in the Roman Empire died, including many Christians who stayed to care for the sick.[27] In the centuries since then, believers have fought against the slave trade and slavery itself. We've built hospitals, fed the hungry, and created organizations for good around the world. We can accomplish much for the kingdom when we work toward the same goals at the speed of unity.

HOW DO YOU KNOW?

It's easy to look back on Nazi Germany and think, "Surely those people knew they were following a man who was drunk with power," but they were sure Hitler was the nation's hero. The German people were thrilled to have a leader who inspired them to overcome their painful past. Business leaders may have been skeptical of Hitler at first, but as the economy grew, they became his biggest fans. Strikingly, most of the pastors and church leaders closed their eyes to the racial hatred spewing from his lips because the country was stable and prosperous again.

Okay, it's unlikely that anyone reading this book is going to take over a country and use power to start a war and kill millions, but we can use the speed of unity for good or ill in our contexts. So how do you know if your motives are right?

In the church world, pastors can be as competitive as any business leader. One pastor said that when he goes to pastors conferences, he observes that attendees are constantly checking to see where they are on the pecking order of success. Their measuring sticks are attendance, the size of buildings, and contributions. It takes large doses of inner confidence and humility to fight against the temptation of comparison.

I BELIEVE PEOPLE HAVE TWO SETS OF WIRING: SELFISH AND SELFLESS. THE ONE THAT IS HOOKED UP TO THE SOURCE OF ENERGY IS THE ONE THAT POWERS THE PERSON.

Not all businesses are motivated exclusively by profits, market share, and share price. "Success" can be more noble than numbers. I believe people have two sets of wiring: selfish and selfless. The one that is hooked up to the source of energy is the one that powers the person. The best business leaders believe they're making a difference in the lives of people, and their passion is directed toward them even more than making a ton of money.

In an article about motives of leaders in business, Lahle Wolfe comments on the nature of passionate, driven entrepreneurs:

> Successful entrepreneurs are rarely motivated solely by money. Successful entrepreneurs achieve wealth because they believe in what they are doing and inject personal core values into how they build a business: Wealth is their reward; not their god.
>
> Having a true sense of pride and belief in your own company and products will convey in everything you do. Your passion and confidence will get other people—customers and investors—excited about the business and you will have an easier time establishing your business' credibility.
>
> If your only goal is to make as much money off other people as fast as you can, eventually you will make business decisions for the wrong reasons and ultimately hurt your reputation and growth potential.[28]

I recommend three practices to keep us on the right path: personal reflection, coaching, and welcoming hard questions.

Practice personal reflection.

Great leaders are activists, but their activities are shaped by spending time alone so they can think honestly and creatively. Is it possible to reflect so much that it gets in the way of getting things done? I guess so, but I don't know anyone who errs on that side of the ledger. Most of us don't carve out time to sit quietly to think. We have goals, we have deadlines, and we have people who are asking for our help. We can't even turn off our phones when we're on a date with our spouse or when we're hanging out with family and friends. In today's culture, people are "always on." We're so connected to our phones that we anticipate getting a call or a text all day every day. It's important—no, it's necessary—for us regularly to shut out the world so we can think, plan, and pray. We'll find plenty of excuses to stay plugged in, but we need to resist them.

Others of us are willing to reflect, but we spend virtually all of our time plotting strategies for the next program or event. That's important, but even more, we need to ask ourselves the big questions, the "why" questions that force us to analyze our motives. We can't change what we don't see, and honest reflection helps us see the truth that's in our souls. We're all a mixed bag of pure and impure motives. We won't have completely pure motives until we see Jesus, but even now, we can make choices to do the right things for the right reasons.

People have different motivations for reading the Bible. Some read to prepare for a sermon, some study for inspiration, and still others read because it's a good habit, but we're wise to read with the expectation that God will break through the haze and actually speak to us. That's the promise of the writer to the Hebrews: "For the word of God is alive and powerful. It is sharper than the sharpest two-edged sword, cutting between soul and spirit, between joint and marrow. It exposes our innermost thoughts and desires. Nothing in all creation is hidden from

God. Everything is naked and exposed before his eyes, and he is the one to whom we are accountable" (Hebrews 4:12-13).

Read Scripture, listen, and expect God to refine why you do what you do. He loves you more than you can possibly know, and He wants you to serve Him with all your heart, no matter what kind of work you do.

GREAT COACHES HELP US ADDRESS SPECIFIC MANAGEMENT ISSUES SUCH AS PLANNING AND PERSONNEL, BUT THEY ALSO ADDRESS MATTERS OF THE HEART: OUR MOTIVES.

Find a coach.

I'm a big fan of coaching. I've been on the receiving end of input and feedback from tremendously insightful people, and I coach some young leaders. Working with a coach, however, isn't magic. It takes time, intention, and effort to get the most out of the relationship. We need to interview prospective coaches to be sure the person can provide what we need, and we need an agreement about the time, the cost, and the expected outcomes. As the relationship grows, a good chemistry should develop. Trust is gradually strengthened, and we become increasingly open to the coach's input. Great coaches help us address specific management issues such as planning and personnel, but they also address matters of the heart: our motives. They know that misguided motives add strain to everything we do. We may be working like crazy, but we enjoy it less and less, and our hyper-intensity drives off the best people. A coach will occasionally ask if our highest hope is to build a big tower with the goal of calling attention to ourselves, and we need to be honest about our answer.

Be open to hard questions.

Driven, assertive people are always on the move, eager to accomplish the next goal. They don't want anyone or anything to slow them down, but wise leaders are willing to invite people to ask hard questions. Who asks these questions? Team members and coaches are usually on the front line with us, so they have the best access. Board members are looking at things from a higher perspective, and they may address issues we haven't considered. Customers and parishioners often ask very profound questions. But in my life, the person whose questions are most often on target (and hardest to escape) is Becca. A spouse has a ringside seat to our lives and sees when our defenses are down. We may try to ignore the penetrating questions (and maybe deflect them with a snarky comment or two), but we're smart to listen, engage in conversation, and discover the truth about why we do what we do.

PAY ATTENTION

The speed of unity can be used by organizations of every size and purpose for good, including churches, parachurch organizations, businesses, and political parties. But we see the power of unity misused in groups like office cliques, the incredibly evil Ku Klux Klan, the destructive communism of the Soviet Union, China, and North Korea, and some political movements in our own country. In subtle or blatant ways, leaders can give in to the temptation to build big towers to make their names great. If that's you, recognize it, admit it, and fight it.

Replace those motives with the passion to make a difference in the lives of others.

Whether you serve in the church or in business, look to the one who had the highest goals and the purest motives. In *The Irresistible Revolution,* Shane Claiborne reminds us, "Only Jesus would be crazy enough to suggest that if you want to become the greatest, you should become the least. Only Jesus would declare God's blessing on the poor rather than on the rich and would insist that it's not enough to just love your friends. I just began to wonder if anybody still believed Jesus meant those things he said."[29]

I do. Do you?

THINK ABOUT IT:

1. What do some leaders (and maybe you and I) hope will be the emotional, relational, and vocational payoff of building a big tower to make themselves look great?

2. What are the payoffs of having a higher purpose of honoring God and serving people? What are the challenges?

3. It's easy to think the German people were fools for following Hitler, but that's hindsight. What do you think made him so attractive to so many?

4. What are the effects of the "always on" culture on your family, friends, and coworkers? What are the effects on you?

5. Take some time now to examine the real reasons you do what you do. Write what you learned and what you're going to do about it.

CHAPTER 8

YOU'LL KNOW IT WHEN YOU FEEL IT

God is looking for those with whom He can do the impossible—what a pity that we plan only the things that we can do by ourselves.

A. W. TOZER

When I speak on the speed of unity, one of the most common (and most important) questions people ask is, "How will I know when we're there? What are the markers that show my team is moving at the speed of unity?"

My answer may not satisfy those who are very concrete in their thinking, but most leaders and team members resonate with my words: "You'll know it when you feel it." When a team is moving at the speed of unity, it's unmistakable . . . almost tangible. There's an electricity in the air . . . a sense of camaraderie that we're all pulling together . . . and the belief that nothing is impossible.

Almost all of us have had the experience of walking into a restaurant and sensing that something isn't right. We don't have to see that they failed the city health inspection. It may be clean, and the food may be very good, but there's a vibe in the air among the staff that they're not rowing in the same direction. But we've also walked into a restaurant and sensed the warmth and joy of the staff. They actually enjoy waiting on us! The food may not be any better than the other restaurant, but that's okay. We feel relaxed, and we can delight in every moment.

We can't achieve the speed of unity simply by changing the organizational chart or having a weekend away. It happens when hearts are melted by love and melded by the common commitment to the greater vision. Unity has always been a goal of leadership and a means of accomplishing something great. When God's people approached the Temple in Jerusalem on one of their holidays, they sang:

> How wonderful and pleasant it is
> when brothers live together in harmony!
> For harmony is as precious as the anointing oil
> that was poured over Aaron's head,
> that ran down his beard
> and onto the border of his robe.
> Harmony is as refreshing as the dew from Mount Hermon
> that falls on the mountains of Zion.
> And there the Lord has pronounced his blessing,
> even life everlasting. (Psalm 133)

I'm not suggesting you dump a quart of canola oil on your head. The image there is of a leader who is demonstrating his commitment to a purpose far higher than his own comfort, prestige, control, or acclaim. Paradoxically, this kind of unity always has a purpose higher, wider, and deeper than the team or group. In an arid land, the love of people is like the heavy dew that nourishes the forests and fields. In the same way, in the dog-eat-dog world of business, supportive relationships nourish the hearts of those involved, and they provide the energy and creativity to accomplish great things in the community. Both are parts of the blessing . . . a blessing that's more felt than measured.

If you want your business, church, or nonprofit to move at top speed, don't stop until you feel it. You'll never want to go back again. The sixth sense that the team has a powerful unity is the primary tell, but let me give you a few more benchmarks.

IF YOU WANT YOUR BUSINESS, CHURCH, OR NONPROFIT TO MOVE AT TOP SPEED, DON'T STOP UNTIL YOU FEEL IT. YOU'LL NEVER WANT TO GO BACK AGAIN.

CERTAIN SIGNS

How can we know we're shifting into the speed of unity? Here are some signs:

We get a lift, not a letdown.

On teams that are at the speed of agreement (or in reverse), people often form cliques to align themselves against others, but these aren't positive alliances. Their motive may be survival in a hostile environment, but this type of unity creates greater disunity as people outside the circle feel alienated and condemned. Shared contempt isn't the speed of unity! When these people see those who aren't in their clique, they feel disgusted . . . and it shows on their faces.

When I have an unresolved conflict with someone, and I see that person at a ball game or a restaurant, I immediately have a physical reaction: my eyes dart away (and I try to act like I didn't see him), I turn my back, my jaw gets tense, and I feel it in the pit of my stomach . . . but maybe it's just me. This isn't a new reaction. When I was a kid and disobeyed my parents, I did everything possible to avoid being in the room with them, and made sure our eyes never met.

When you see people on your team, do you avoid eye contact? Do you roll your eyes? Do your shoulders get tense? Do you get a knot in your stomach? Do you hurry your walk so they can't catch up with you or walk the other way to avoid them entirely? Or do you get a surge of affection and enthusiasm because you feel supported?

At the speed of unity, when I see someone on the team, I get a lift. Trust, hope, and genuine love make us glad to see each other, and we're eager to tackle the next task together. I think, *I'm so glad she's on the team. I'm thrilled that he brings his best every day. I hope they stay with us a long time. I can't wait to hear the latest news about her family.* And if I hear someone on the team is struggling with a problem, my thoughts don't go to condemnation and blame, but instead, I want to ask, "How can I help?"

Letdown or lift—it's not that hard to identify our reactions to people on the team.

We don't second-guess each other.

Have you ever been on a team when you were afraid to give a report because you knew you'd be grilled about every detail? I have, and it was incredibly draining. I was always on edge, ready to defend myself against all comers. In this environment, even normal, benign questions are interpreted as attacks.

What is second-guessing about? We openly wonder about a person's competence, loyalty, or motives to put them down and appear superior to them. Because they offended us, we want to punish them and make them look foolish—and this is a way to get revenge. Do you think that's too harsh? I assure you it's true.

When a team is moving at the speed of unity, people don't second-guess each other. This means they don't pick things apart or have an attitude of superiority, and they don't question each other's motives. I'm not saying that questions are out of bounds. Actually, in a positive, supportive atmosphere, we're more open to hard questions because we don't feel the need to protect ourselves. We can answer honestly without fear of ridicule.

We laugh *with* each other and even *at* each other.

Pastors and business leaders often talk about their teams being a family, but for lots of us, that's a pretty low bar! Many families are anything but unified. In fact, that's where we learned the fine art of avoiding hard discussions and intimidating people. We spent our time blaming others and second-guessing ourselves. At every moment, someone had to be blamed for all the craziness! We laughed, but either as a release of all the tension or with the edge of scorn at someone's mistake. We laughed as we made sarcastic remarks, but that's passive-aggressive—we wanted to put people down and still be able to say, "Hey, I was only kidding!" But the message was very clear to the target and everyone else that we'll use our tongues to inflict damage.

One of the most beautiful signs of moving at the speed of unity is when people from painful, manipulative backgrounds feel so affirmed and secure that the way they relate to others is radically changed. They no longer feel the need to fight, flee, or freeze when there's even the slightest disagreement. Instead, they can relax, laugh at themselves, and laugh with others.

Instead of being defensive when we fail, we don't take ourselves so seriously, and in really unified teams, we tell stories about our blunders so others can join in the laughter. As a solid foundation of trust gradually erodes the need for self-protection, genuine love relieves the pressure to defend and pose. On teams like this, people have a beautiful blend of enjoyment and drive.

We cry with each other.

At the lower gears, a person's tears get in the way of transactions and accomplishments. In those organizations, a few people may have empathy for those who are hurting, but others see their pain as an unnecessary and unwanted distraction. Some people feel uncomfortable with those who express heartache, and they avoid them at all costs, but others who feel just as uncomfortable rush in to fix the problem. They may appear noble, but their real goals are to control the situation so they feel more stable and win applause for being a hero.

How can we identify real empathy? From my perspective, it's when we move toward a person who is struggling and listen, really listen. Instead of offering quick and simple solutions to often very complex problems, we say, "Tell me more about that," or "Help me understand what's going on." We may notice that a person's reaction is disproportional to the event—over-the-top anger, fear, tears, or some other expression of emotion. In this case, being exasperated and saying, "Stop that!" won't elicit a positive response! Extreme expressions of emotions are almost always a sign that "there's an issue under the issue." The deeper issue needs to be addressed at some point, but probably not immediately. When the time is right, share your observations and explore the underlying source of the powerful emotions, or when you uncover them, suggest a counselor who has more experience in resolving them. Some problems are best left to professionals.

Empathy isn't important only in the most tragic moments; it's part of the fabric of a team that's moving at the speed of unity. When people feel understood, relationships grow stronger, failure isn't as much of a threat, and people have the freedom to learn and grow at their own pace. We laugh with each other, but we also cry with each other. We might assume church teams measure much higher on this scale than business teams, but that's not always the case. This level of caring takes time and effort; it means we move beyond transactional relationships, and we value each person.

We hear it.

What does the team celebrate? And how do they celebrate? One of the marks of a team running at top speed is that people are as excited about another person's success as they are about their own. I watch people celebrate another's achievement, and at the speed of unity, their clapping and cheering is sincere, not forced or fake. At the lower speeds, a person who isn't in alignment with the team stands reluctantly and gives a couple of polite golf claps.

As we've seen, the speed of unity isn't a zero-sum game—that is, one person's success doesn't diminish anyone else. It's not "I win, you lose." Instead, it's "I win, we win" and "You win, we win."

When a team is in top gear, the language of unity pours out of each person. When Jesus' adversaries tried to condemn Him with harsh accusations, He put them in their place when He told them, "For out of the abundance of the heart, the mouth speaks" (Matthew 12:34 WEB). In the negative sense, those who are looking out only for themselves use people as steppingstones to personal success. They resent anyone else getting applause, and their words reveal their hearts: fiercely competitive, putting people down, calling attention to their success, using sarcasm to punish, and similar messages. But the hearts of people who are unified are secure, so faith, hope, and love spill from their mouths.

Oh, they can be very analytical, but their examination is designed to make progress, not to find fault and crush the person.

Have you listened to a band when the guitars weren't in tune, the person at the keyboard was off beat, and the drummer lost one of his sticks? That's what a team sounds like when they aren't unified. They argue, but without trust or the hope of finding a common resolution; they insist on their own way and defy anyone to disagree; and they either don't realize they're so out of tune (because that's the only thing they've ever heard) or they don't have the skills or confidence to wade in and do the hard work of getting everyone in tune.

As we've seen, unified teams "speak the language" and "sing the song." Their messages to each other and those outside the team are consistent, positive, and powerful. They aren't robots who don't believe what they're saying. Quite the opposite: they've bought into the mission, and they want to communicate the message as loudly and clearly as possible.

We accomplish more than we could do individually.

It's intuitively obvious that teams whose members encourage each other will be more successful than those that are full of people who are out for themselves. That's certainly my experience in different churches and as I've watched businesses and other organizations. But you don't have to take my word for it. In an article in the *Harvard Business Review,* the author cites research published by the *Journal of Applied Behavioral Science,* which found that "a workplace characterized by positive and virtuous practices excels in a number of domains." These practices include:

- Caring for, being interested in, and maintaining responsibility for colleagues as friends.
- Providing support for one another, including offering kindness and compassion when others are struggling.

- Avoiding blame and forgiving mistakes.
- Inspiring one another at work.
- Emphasizing the meaningfulness of the work.
- Treating one another with respect, gratitude, trust, and integrity.

The author of the study concludes: "When organizations institute positive, virtuous practices they achieve significantly higher levels of organizational effectiveness—including financial performance, customer satisfaction, and productivity . . . The more the virtuousness, the higher the performance in profitability, productivity, customer satisfaction, and employee engagement."[30] In other words, the research published in these prestigious journals found that teams that move at the speed of unity achieve greater success.

IN OTHER WORDS, THE RESEARCH PUBLISHED IN THESE PRESTIGIOUS JOURNALS FOUND THAT TEAMS THAT MOVE AT THE SPEED OF UNITY ACHIEVE GREATER SUCCESS.

OPTIONAL?

When I've taught about the speed of unity, some people roll their eyes—not in disgust, but because they can't imagine it. All they've ever known was the speed of agreement and the speed of vision, and it has taken everything they've got to run at those speeds. If I can read their faces, they're telling me, "Yeah, that sounds great, Rob, but we're doing the best we can already. I'm not up for adding some new benchmarks to our goals."

I understand. I've been there. Frankly, I'm one of those who shrugged when I heard leaders talk about unity because I was sure the necessary traits were unachievable and irreconcilable polar opposites: unity and drive, caring and accomplishing, empathy and goals. But I was wrong. As I thought more about the importance of unity, I remembered Jesus' prayer just before He was arrested, tried, convicted, and executed. John gives us a front row seat to watch and listen to Jesus as He poured out His heart to the Father. Near the end of this beautiful prayer, He prayed for us: "I have given them the glory you gave me, so they may be one as we are one. I am in them and you are in me. May they experience such perfect unity that the world will know that you sent me and that you love them as much as you love me" (John 17:22-23).

Jesus didn't tell us to do great things and say, "Good luck!" He gave us His glory. That means He revealed himself to us in power, mercy, grace, forgiveness, and joy, and He wants us to experience all He has for us. His heart and His excellence are not just for each of us individually; He wants us to "be one" with each other. How much? As much as He is one with the Father! Only when we experience "such perfect unity" can we be the people God wants us to be and do the great things He wants us to do. In the mind and heart of Jesus, unity isn't optional.

SO . . . WHAT ABOUT YOU?

Be honest about where you are. If you and your team are moving at the speed of agreement, take the necessary steps to craft a vision that gets you up in the morning. And if you've been moving at the speed of vision, you can shift gears and go much faster and farther. If you've read this chapter and you realize the description of what it feels like to run at top gear fits like a glove, that's fantastic! But if you don't feel it, don't kid yourself. The longer you tell yourself something that isn't true, the more you'll believe the lie.

BE HONEST ABOUT WHERE YOU ARE.

Of course, it takes time to shift gears from one speed to another, so voicing the desire to move at the speed of unity is only the first step. As you shift into this gear, you'll gradually gain speed as you and your team become more unified, rub the rough spots off each other, quickly and graciously address anyone who gets out of alignment, and fine-tune your engine.

When you've tasted the sweetness and success of the speed of unity, you'll never settle for anything less. It'll change you, how you lead and follow, how you relate to your family, and how you anticipate the future. You'll never want to lose it . . . and you'll always want to protect it.

THINK ABOUT IT:

1. Describe a time when you walked into a restaurant or a business and something just felt wrong. And describe a time when it felt right. What are some differences?

2. Do you lean toward concrete thinking or intuition? How would your cognitive "bent" shape how you interpret the signs of the speed of unity described in this chapter?

3. On a scale of 0 (not in the least) to 10 (all day every day), rate your team's chemistry according to the traits in this chapter.

___We get a lift, not a letdown.

___We don't second-guess each other.

___We laugh with and even at each other.

___We cry with each other.

___We hear it.

___We accomplish more than we could do individually.

What does this analysis tell you about your team?

4. Do you think the others on your team genuinely believe you "have their backs"? Are you convinced they have your back? Explain your answer.

5. Have you viewed unity as optional (or even a distraction)? Explain your answer.

CHAPTER 9

PROTECT UNITY

We are only as strong as we are united, as weak as we are divided.

***ALBUS DUMBLEDORE ADDRESSING THE STUDENTS OF HOGWARTS, J.K. ROWLING,* HARRY POTTER AND THE GOBLET OF FIRE**

What are the two most important instruments in a rock band? (Yeah, I know I'm throwing you a curve here, but go with me.) Do you know? It's the bass guitar and the drums. If the keyboard is off, listeners will only think the pianist is adding a taste of jazz. And if the lead guitar is a hair off, they assume he's creative. But the bass and the drums have to be "in the pocket" or people will want to stick their fingers in their ears. If the band is out of sync, even the songs you've looked forward to hearing make you feel like somebody is scratching fingernails on a blackboard or a tire is out of balance as you drive on the highway. It's horrible! It doesn't take a professional musician to notice; everybody knows it. Those two musicians, the bass player and the drummer, hold everything together so the tune sounds right. The unity of the band—and the rightness of the rhythm—depends on two key members.

What does this have to do with the speed of unity in a business, a church, or a nonprofit organization? Everything! Like the band, keeping the team in tune with each other so the music they make is beautiful and powerful is in the hands of one person—the leader . . . maybe you.

If you're the leader of a team on any level, from the executive team or board to the grassroots teams, you're responsible to be in alignment with the vision and values of the organization. If you're out of rhythm, your team will be out of rhythm. You set the pace, you establish the beat, your attitude and actions are the rhythm of the team. They're looking to you to keep them unified in their purpose and processes, and if anyone is out of sync, it's your job to get them back in rhythm. You do that by continually reminding people of the values, reinforcing the direction, reiterating the vision, affirming people who are with you, and correcting those who are out of sync—preferably before anyone else follows their lead.

Usually, we have to listen closely to hear the first notes that lose the rhythm, but sometimes it's like a cannon going off in the middle of a symphony. Years ago, I led a reorganization, and in a staff meeting, I explained the new reporting structure. As I looked around the room, most of the people were either nodding or looked like they were prepared to ask a clarifying question. Then I looked at Julie. (I'm not using her real name, and you'll see why.) As I explained the new system, she slowly and deliberately pulled her long hair around to cover her face. (I'm not kidding.) When I first noticed, she had only a few wisps there, but soon, her face was entirely veiled by her hair. I'm not a psychologist, but it doesn't take one to realize her actions were a loud and clear message that she wanted to hide . . . in plain sight!

I tried like crazy to keep my train of thought and continue explaining the details of the new reporting structure, but it was impossible. I was totally distracted, and so was everybody else in the room. None of us could believe this was happening! Every pair of eyes in the room (except Julie's, of course) darted between Julie and me to see what I was going to do. Would I protect the unity of our team, or would I be so flustered that I bailed out at this important moment?

Thankfully, it was a few minutes before noon. I told the team, "It's about time for lunch. All of you can go, but Julie, I'd like you to stay behind and talk with me."

After everybody had left, Julie and I were alone in the room. I said, "Julie, it appears you feel uncomfortable with the assignment of whom you will report to. You haven't said anything, but what you've done with your hair speaks loudly and clearly to me." I paused for a few seconds to let my observation sink in. "If you don't mind, please put your hair back so we can see each other." She haltingly reached up and swept her hair back over her head. She obviously still didn't want to look at me, but I continued, "I need to protect the unity of the team. You've been passive-aggressive and inappropriate. When we get to the restaurant for lunch, you need to apologize to the team. I'm going to give you five minutes. Anytime during the first five minutes, you can interrupt me and apologize to everyone. If you don't, I'll make the apology for you, and then later, you and I will have another conversation—a much more pointed conversation. Do you understand?" She nodded and got up to go to lunch.

When we arrived at the restaurant, I gave Julie five minutes, along with thirty seconds of added grace, but she didn't look up the whole time. I stopped what I was talking about and said, "Let me stop for a minute. I have something important to say. On behalf of Julie, I want to apologize to all of you for her passive-aggressive behavior in our meeting this morning. You noticed it. I noticed it. I talked to her about it, and she and I will have another conversation later today." Then I proceeded with the staff lunch and told everyone to enjoy the meal. Julie had been anxious and defensive before, but she was sweating bullets now!

Later that afternoon, I asked Julie to come to my office. She still wouldn't look at me. I told her, "I gave you an opportunity to make things right with the team, and you chose not to do it. It's my role to protect the unity of our team, and your actions were disruptive. If you had apologized and realigned yourself with us, we wouldn't be having this conversation. But you didn't. I can't have you on the team any longer. I'll let you decide if you want to resign or be let go."

She quickly said, "You can let me go."

I shook my head, "Let's try it again: you can resign and leave with some dignity, or I can let you go."

Her voice was barely audible: "Please, just let me go."

Had she been out of tune with our team before that day? Maybe, but I didn't see it. When I saw it, I had to do something about it. I gave her the chance to make things right, but for whatever reason, she chose to stay out of sync with us—permanently.

I wish I could say the situation with Julie is unique for River Valley, but it's not. I've made dozens of minor adjustments to get people back in rhythm with the "band," and a few as dramatic as the one with Julie. Several years ago, two guys on our team, I'll call them Pete and Scott, had gotten under each other's skin. For a few weeks in staff meetings, I began to notice sarcastic remarks and other kinds of digs . . . and they gradually escalated. At first, I thought they were just having fun with each other the way a lot of brothers do, but after a few weeks (yeah, I'm slow), I realized their barbs weren't all that good-natured after all. They privately griped to me about each other, and they tried to get others on the team allied with them against the other. In our staff meetings, they rolled their eyes or made obnoxious sounds like a horse at any comment the other made, and the words between them were meant to cut like a razor. They were trying to destroy each other in front of their peers!

I tried a remedy similar to the one I used with Julie. I ended the meeting by saying, "Okay, that's it for today. You can leave . . . except for Pete and Scott. I want to talk to the two of you."

After everybody left, I looked them in the eyes and said sternly, "This is Tuesday. I'm giving you until Friday to sort things out, forgive each other, and find a way to love each other—not tolerate each other, but love each other. And if you don't, both of you will be fired."

Instantly, both of them tried to argue their case by blaming the other. I held up my hand and barked, "Stop! Don't talk to me. You don't have a problem with me. You have a problem with each other. You need to talk to each other to make this right. I want both of you in my office at 9:00 on Friday morning. If you don't love each other by then, you're gone."

At that hour on Friday, the two of them strolled into my office smiling and patting each other on the back. They had become best friends! It was obvious they weren't faking it. I didn't have to ask a single question. Scott blurted out, "We got together Tuesday afternoon to talk about our differences, and we realized we'd made a lot of unfair assumptions. Every little thing became a big thing, but at the bottom, we really care about each other."

Pete joined in, "Pastor Rob, we're so sorry for causing such headaches for you and everybody on the team. The next time we're together, we want a few minutes to apologize and tell everybody we've buried the hatchet."

I wish all confrontations turned out like this one.

A SLIPPERY THING

Protecting unity requires us to have hard conversations, demand alignment, and make difficult decisions if people choose disunity. It's always been that way. Unity is a slippery thing, easily lost. In the early years of the Christian faith, the people involved in the church were a varied bunch: former Jewish priests and prostitutes who had come to faith, rich people and slaves, those who had always tried to obey God and those who had never tried at all, insiders and outsiders, the high and the low of their society.

In fact, many of the letters in the New Testament are about healing broken relationships among believers. Paul spent three years in the metropolitan city of Ephesus, so he knew the flash points of disagreement and conflict among the Christians there. Later, when he wrote to them, he explained that a genuine experience of God's love and grace is the only sure way for love to flow from us to others, and he gave them this instruction: "Be completely humble and gentle; be patient, bearing with one another in love. Make every effort to keep the unity of the Spirit through the bond of peace" (Ephesians 4:2-3 NIV). Don't miss it: "Make every effort to keep the unity." Being united in heart is a "sacred oneness" that's enormously precious but very fragile. Paul was very well aware that unity doesn't come naturally. We have to experience love so we can express it, and we have to experience security so we can create a dynamically positive culture.

If you're a leader, you're the bass player or the drummer. It's your responsibility to "make every effort to keep the unity" of your team.

"LEAD LIKE YOU PARENT"

One day a number of years ago, before my conversations with Julie, Pete, and Scott, I prayed for our team and sensed God tell me, "Pastor like you parent." Since many of the leaders reading this book aren't pastors, I'll change it to "Lead like you parent." Instantly, I knew exactly what He was saying to me. In my relationships with my sons, I do my best to give them what some experts call "roots and wings," a deep sense of security in my strong and unending love, and the encouragement to fly, to take risks without the fear of being ridiculed for failure. I'm always willing to wade in when I sense Logan or Connor is out of alignment with our family values because my goal is for them to flourish, but I had been avoiding hard conversations with our staff members because my goal with them was different: to avoid the messiness of conflict. I sensed God say to me, "Do you want the people on your team to feel so secure that they're eager to do anything and everything to fulfill My vision, or do you just want to steer clear of conversations that make you feel uncomfortable?"

I SENSED GOD SAY TO ME, "DO YOU WANT THE PEOPLE ON YOUR TEAM TO FEEL SO SECURE THAT THEY'RE EAGER TO DO ANYTHING AND EVERYTHING TO FULFILL MY VISION, OR DO YOU JUST WANT TO STEER CLEAR OF CONVERSATIONS THAT MAKE YOU FEEL UNCOMFORTABLE?"

Ouch. That was a turning point for me and my leadership. I told God, "Okay, I'll do it. Whenever I see one of our people out of alignment, I'll speak the truth in love because I care more about the opportunities in their future than avoiding uncomfortable conversations in the present."

Good parents are intentional with their kids—not smothering them with attention or demands, but learning the skills of parenting so we give them plenty of love and increasing freedom to make their own decisions as they mature and prove they're aligned with our hearts and vision. That's the kind of leader God wants me to be with our staff members.

I hope I haven't given you the impression in earlier chapters that moving at the speed of unity is easy, effortless, and totally free from conflict. It's not. Spoiler alert: As our unity has grown on our team, we've experienced *more* friction, but it's good and productive friction. Because we have unity, people feel more comfortable disagreeing with each other because disagreement isn't a threat to their sense of personal value or their place on the team. Previously, we avoided certain topics or framed particularly delicate issues (like failure) to avoid hurting people's feelings, but now we're much more secure and willing to be honest with each other. When we had less unity, we were polite but guarded . . . and insincere. As our unity quotient has risen, we feel more comfortable being honest with each other. Has that produced tension? Yes, but it's creative tension . . . which is a world away from destructive, passive-aggressive behavior that's the norm for teams at lower gears.

SHIELDS AND SWORDS

To protect the unity of our team, I need to pick up two pieces of armor: a shield to ward off attacks and a sword to cut to the heart of each person on the team. Great leaders develop particular skills to protect their team's unity. Here are some I've been working on:

Ask better questions.

I don't make as many assumptions as I once did. When I sense a problem, I'm much quicker to say, "Hey, tell me what's going on here." And as the conversation develops, I've learned to ask better questions to get to the heart of things. Instead of letting people get away with shifting blame, I often ask, "So, what's your responsibility in all this? What are you going to do to make it right even if nobody else takes a step?"

Give honor in all directions.

In many organizations, the boss or the pastor gets the lion's share of accolades. This feeds the leader's ego, but it has detrimental effects on other people: they may be driven to succeed so they can receive applause, they may try to sabotage those who are climbing higher than them, or they may give up and become passive. In equal measure, we need to honor people up the ladder, those who are peers, and those who report to us. In fact, I've come to the conclusion that unity is created and protected most powerfully when I honor the people at the very bottom of the organizational chart. Their contributions may go unnoticed by most people, but their faithfulness and skills are the foundation of our growth. We couldn't do what we do without them, and I want them—and everybody else—to know it.

Forgive quickly and thoroughly.

Everybody makes mistakes, and everybody can be selfish. In organizations that are moving at the speeds of agreement and vision, failures are big threats, but not at the speed of unity. As we've seen, we can learn the invaluable art of treating people the way we want to be treated: forgiving as we hope to be forgiven, loving as we want to be loved, and accepting people who are very different from us in the same way we long to be accepted.

FORGIVENESS IS AT THE HEART OF THE CHRISTIAN FAITH, AND IT'S AT THE HEART OF TEAMS THAT MOVE AT THE SPEED OF UNITY.

Forgiveness is at the heart of the Christian faith, and it's at the heart of teams that move at the speed of unity. We can create an environment so that forgiving people who have offended us isn't rare or awkward, but instead, it's normal and freeing. But many people, including many Christians who are leaders in business and the church, make one of two mistakes in forgiveness: they forgive too soon or too late. We forgive too soon when we quickly say, "No problem," when we excuse the person by saying, "Oh, he couldn't help it," or when we minimize the damage and declare, "It really didn't hurt me that much. I'm fine." No, forgiveness requires us to be honest about the pain we've experienced. On the other end of the spectrum, some people forgive too late, which means not at all. They feel their resentment is completely valid, and it gives them two things they value: an identity as "the one who was wronged" and an adrenaline rush of energy that comes with harboring anger.

It seems noble to insist that we would say, "It didn't bother me," or "He couldn't help it," but that only lets our anger simmer—and eventually, it boils over. When that happens, we can't stand being in the same room with the person. We may be on the same team, but we're not for that person at all. Instead of loving and supporting each other, we create distance, we resent, and we try to hurt the person through passive-aggressive gossip or direct aggression. (Most Christians take the passive-aggressive approach.) But wanting the other person to suffer is a form of revenge, and the desire for revenge is the opposite of forgiveness.

If we don't forgive little offenses, they accumulate and become really big deals. Before long, even the slightest new offense feels traumatic. Author and pastor Lewis Smedes has written, "When we forgive evil we do not excuse it, we do not tolerate it, we do not smother it. We look the evil full in the face, call it what it is, let its horror shock and stun and enrage us, and only then do we forgive it."[31] Do you think the word "evil" is too strong to describe what can happen on staff teams? It's not. I've seen it, and it's ugly. Be honest and dig deep into the grace of God so you can forgive quickly and thoroughly.

An apology is an important first step, but it's not the same thing as forgiveness. We can apologize but secretly hope the person pays for what he's done to us. When we apologize to one another, we stay together, and when we forgive one another, we stay healthy.

Follow the prompts.

Whenever you feel an interior nudge—whether you call it your conscience or the Holy Spirit—to affirm someone, apologize to someone you've offended, forgive someone who has offended you, or give honor to someone publicly, do it. Don't wait. Don't come up with excuses why you shouldn't. Just do it. I'm convinced a lot of us are simply out of practice in responding to these nudges. We can do it. At the speed of unity, we will do it.

Celebrate each other.

No golf claps allowed! At the speed of unity, one person's success is everyone's success. All of us are well aware of the damage and division caused by jealousy. Our solution isn't to grit our teeth and try hard to avoid being snarky. The solution is to value each person's talents and contribution as much as your own, and to be thrilled when others excel. When others' success is a threat, the team can't move at the speed of unity, but when we genuinely celebrate with each other, we can fly!

No side talks.

I've seen it, you've seen it, we've all seen it: a person on the team isn't happy about a decision or a direction, but instead of speaking up in the group, he waits until later to meet privately with a person he thinks will be his ally. This is a natural and normal way people try to gain support, but it's deadly to a team that wants to move at the speed of unity.

Speak up, not out.

This is a corollary of no side talk. When people on the team have a problem with the leader, they need to speak up and voice their concerns—to the leader, not to people outside the team. I've seen incredible destruction from a team member "sharing" with people who have no direct knowledge of the context of a decision and are only hearing one side. Secret alliances give us a thrill, and we appreciate the unquestioning support we may get, but each of these conversations is a spike in the heart of the team.

Pray for each person.

If you're a person of faith, you know the importance of prayer. When we talk to God, we tap into the greatest source of love, wisdom, and power in the universe. And when we talk to Him, we open our hearts for Him to work in us to make us better leaders. Prayer—real prayer—takes time and intention. A few quick words don't cut it. We're bringing ourselves, our team, and our concerns "boldly to the throne of our gracious God. There we will receive his mercy, and we will find grace to help us when we need it most" (Hebrews 4:16).

As we've seen, Jesus prayed for unity for His followers. Maybe it would be a good idea for us as leaders to pray for unity among our followers in the company, the team, the church, or the organization.

Stay in the flow.

We're busy. We carry heavy loads of responsibility. People are pulling us in every direction. It's easy to react to the flashing red lights and make those pressures our highest priorities. I get it, but when we're running so hard that we're often disengaged from the team, the other members gradually lose passion and energy. I'm not saying we have to be there every minute of every day. I travel away from Minneapolis quite a bit to speak at events, but I try to be sure to be with our team if at all possible.

At the speed of unity, we don't find excuses to avoid people on the team. We're drawn to be with them because it's fun, encouraging, stimulating, and exciting! Of course, we're thoroughly human, and sometimes we're exhausted and we just don't want to be with anybody, even the people on our team. But it's important to stay in the flow—not just in body, but in mind and spirit, too, to be fully present in our time together.

THE INVESTMENT

I could tell you that when you make a few decisions to move from the speed of vision to the speed of unity that everything will easily fall into place, but that's not true. The transition from second gear to top gear chews up a leader's bandwidth. The inherent question is simple: is it worth the effort?

Years ago, an automotive parts company ran a television commercial with a mechanic standing next to a car with the hood up. He held up an oil filter and smiled, "You can pay me now," then he picked up a piston and growled, "or you can pay me later." It was obvious that he was talking about the difference between the price of an oil filter and an engine overhaul. It's the same calculation for leaders: we can pay a relatively small price of time and energy to shift gears to the speed of unity, or we'll spend far more leadership capital trying to keep things running at the speed of agreement or vision—constantly dealing with conflict, misalignment, hurt feelings, and wasted effort.

Let me use a different analogy: The largest rocket in the SpaceX line is called Falcon Heavy. It has external boosters and internal engines. It expends tremendous energy to get into space. The boosters burn for only 154 seconds on liquid oxygen, blasting off and shaking the ground around the launchpad. When the boosters are spent and fall off a few miles up, the first stage burns for 187 seconds. When that fuel is spent, the second stage burns for 397 seconds. Together, the boosters and first two stages burn an enormous amount of fuel to get the Falcon Heavy and its payload into space. But here's the point: once it's beyond earth's atmosphere, the payload in the capsule is moving at an incredible speed in the weightlessness of space, and it can be maneuvered with only puffs of energy.

Don't be surprised that it takes so much of your energy to get beyond the atmosphere and gravity of the lower speeds. You'll need to burn a lot of personal fuel to align your team, offboard a few, onboard some, clarify values, create a culture of love and creativity, and shift into top gear. But when you and your team are running fast in the speed of unity, it only takes small corrections to keep the pace. Don't give up when it takes more of you than you initially expected. You'll be glad you hung in there.

At the speed of unity, problems surface more visibly than at lower speeds. The reason is that everyone on the team is moving together, working like a well-oiled machine, and when someone isn't in alignment, it's plain to the leader and everyone on the team. Instead of ignoring the person and the problem, catch it early, deal with it decisively, offer a path forward for the person, appreciate it when there's a positive response, and move them along if they choose to stay out of alignment. When we protect unity, the people on our teams trust us even more. When one of the people on our team chose to stay out of alignment after I gave him plenty of chances to change, it was time for him to go. This two-week process was gut-wrenching, but when it was over, our team was more unified than ever. The rest of my team appreciated my commitment to unity. One of them told me, "Pastor Rob, I loved you before, but I'd take a bullet for you now!"

Establishing and protecting unity is a new skill set for most leaders. They know how to have transactions with their teams at the speed of agreement, and they're able to paint a compelling picture of the future at the speed of vision, but few have an intrinsic knack to lead at the speed of unity.

The best way to describe the learning curve for most of us is that we have to figure out how to combine the ability to cast vision with the ability to lead like we parent. That's how we protect unity.

THINK ABOUT IT:

1. Why is it important to realize that one person, the leader, is responsible for the rhythm of a team? What happens when a leader doesn't take that role?

2. Who is someone you know who "leads like he or she parents"? What is the impact on the people who follow this person?

3. Have you been on a team when people tried to ignore conflicts? (Of course, you have!) How did it affect you and the chemistry of the team?

4. What are some results—to the offender, the offended, and the team or family—when people forgive too soon? . . . or too late?

5. What are some ways you can tell if unity on a team is threatened?

6. Does the illustration of the fuel necessary to get a rocket into space discourage you or challenge you? Explain your answer.

CHAPTER 10

UNSTOPPABLE

> *But God doesn't call us to be comfortable. He calls us to trust Him so completely that we are unafraid to put ourselves in situations where we will be in trouble if He doesn't come through.*
>
> ***FRANCIS CHAN***

If you've been moving at the speed of agreement or the speed of vision, I hope you see the phenomenal difference it can make to shift into top gear. As I've spoken on this topic to church and business leaders, many have responded, "I love that! Show me how." This book is the "show me how." And some have said, "We've been shifting to the speed of unity, but I didn't have language around it to help my people understand it better. You've given me the terms, concepts, and processes I've needed. Thanks!"

Whatever your current speed, I encourage you to dream bigger. When teams move at the speed of unity, they're unstoppable. I like to say, "*Nothing is impossible* when you're moving at the speed of unity," but you know that I don't mean that you'll be able to reverse gravitational pull or anything like that. I'm talking about fulfilling the amazing potential of the multiplied talents and passion of all the people on your team. I'm sure you want that or you wouldn't have read this far in the book. In fact, our team is working so well together that I'm starting to wonder if my dreams aren't big enough.

BIG DIFFERENCE

When we moved at the speed of vision, we spent a lot of time talking about problems to solve. Today, our team spends much more time focused on the opportunities in the future. Perhaps the primary reason for this shift is that everyone on our team is aligned, equipped, connected, and resourced . . . so they're solving the vast majority of the problems with their teams. All of us experience the benefits.

For me

The speed of unity has freed me up to invest my energies in bigger visions and more expansive goals. It has also freed my heart from the burden of needing to micromanage relationships so small disagreements don't escalate into open conflict.

I NOW HAVE MORE BANDWIDTH FOR CREATIVITY. DREAMING BIG DREAMS IS NO LONGER A LUXURY; IT'S THE NEW NORM.

I now have more bandwidth for creativity. Dreaming big dreams is no longer a luxury; it's the new norm. However, as our team is functioning so well, I can't afford to coast. I'm more motivated than ever to see my leadership skills grow so I can stay one step ahead of these remarkable people.

Paradoxically, even though we're moving at Mach 3, I have more peace than at any time in my career. We're incredibly busy, but we know where we're going, we're going as a team, and we're thrilled to see the impact of our efforts.

At the lower speeds, I enjoyed leading sometimes, but too often it was a grind. (Of course, I hoped nobody would notice that I felt that way!) I carried the burden of success on my shoulders for two reasons: I was convinced that Jim Collins's model of leadership in many companies, "a genius and a thousand helpers," was the right one . . . and I didn't know any other way to lead. But as our team has experienced unity and each person is encouraged to use his or her genius, I thoroughly enjoy leading. I'm like a kid on a carnival ride, grinning from ear to ear at the thrill.

I've talked to dozens of gifted but discouraged leaders in business and the church who have told me their passion has vanished. Many are looking forward to retirement, expecting to feel great relief. But I've also had conversations with a lot of leaders on the other side of retirement, and many of them feel like a ship without a rudder. They long to get back in the game because they want their lives to count. If we want to live with joy and meaning, retirement can't be our primary goal.

I used to daydream about retiring so Becca and I could live on a golf course and I could play every day. But today, I'm not thinking about retirement because I can't imagine anything being more fun and fulfilling than what I'm doing now. My specific role will change when my body can't move at the same pace, but my heart will find a way to keep flying. This isn't a job; it's my life! Leaders whose teams are moving at the speed of agreement use the measuring sticks of personal advancement and income, and when they have enough of both, they get bored out of their minds and they're ready to jump ship. And leaders whose teams are at the speed of vision have an endgame: accomplishing the goal and fulfilling the vision. When that has been achieved, they often feel empty and aimless, and they're ready to go. But when we lead at the speed of unity, the joy, the adventure, and the challenge never end.

For Becca and me

One of the biggest benefits of moving at the speed of unity is in my relationship with Becca. I'm far less preoccupied with problems at the church, so I'm able to give her more attention. When we walk in the mornings, she hears me talk more about possibilities than problems . . . and I listen to her more because I'm not as distracted and consumed by what's going on in the office. Becca and I are more in alignment with each other, with the rest of our family, and with everyone connected to our work. Of course, a pleasant result is that we have more margin. We sleep better, we relax more, we laugh a lot, and we dream together. I'm healthier emotionally, physically, and spiritually because the toxins of fear, hurt, anger, and shame have been minimized . . . and Becca is happier because she doesn't have to figure out how to relate to a crazy man!

For our team

We spent a lot of effort and time to align people on our team, move those who didn't align, enlist competent and passionate people who fit our new culture, and empower them to be and do their best, and it was entirely worth it. The people on our team trust each other, and even more, they like each other! Because they know I trust them, they're secure enough to take greater risks and shoot for the stars. The willingness to take risks is directly related to creativity, and our people come up with amazing ideas. We've moved beyond individual success to celebrate our success as a team. We genuinely cheer each other on. Instead of being driven by pride, fear, and a competitive spirit, we coordinate and cooperate . . . so everybody wins. In other words, no one's success comes at anyone else's expense. Do you think people in the church notice that? Yeah, they do.

For me, for other pastors, and for many leaders in business, all of this has a spiritual component. When we have a sense of God's hand on us as we lead, we function in our "God gear." Our gifts, experience, and love are all energized and directed by God, so our leadership rises to a supernatural level. When we're in alignment with the Spirit of God as we lead, amazing things can happen . . . and do happen.

W³

A year or so ago, a consultant came to River Valley to help us with our branding and marketing. He spent a lot of time trying to understand who we are and why we do what we do. After many conversations, he told me, "I get it. You're a nice guy, but your life is wrapped up in winning. And what's so attractive is that your wins aren't at anyone else's expense. You want to win, you want your team to win, and you want everybody else to win, too. It's like winning to the third power." I like that!

ACTUALLY, AS THE CULTURE OF UNITY BECOMES INGRAINED AT RIVER VALLEY, I ANTICIPATE WINNING TO CONTINUE FOR GENERATIONS TO COME. THAT'S EXPONENTIAL WINNING!

Let me put it in my words: I'm winning as a leader because our team is so effective and it's a joy to work with them; our team is winning because they thrive in an environment of challenge and support; and our broader audience is winning because they get the very best from us. Actually, as the culture of unity becomes ingrained at River Valley, I anticipate winning to continue for generations to come. That's exponential winning!

That's what so many people want to experience. That's why so many join us.

This isn't just a theory, an abstract idea that may be too good to be true. I'm seeing it played out every day in my life, in our family, on our team, and in our church. I see it in the business leaders who have made the shift. I see it in the lives and ministries of pastors we coach around the country and the world.

One of the signs that we're actually running at the speed of unity is that we don't see ourselves in competition with other churches. We're not always checking where we are on the pecking order of size or influence. We don't grimace when they succeed, and we don't secretly celebrate when they struggle. We see them as brothers and sisters who have the same heart, the same passion, and the same goals as ours. In a broader sense, we're on the same team, and we want to move with them at the speed of unity. We're not afraid they'll take people away from us. We're 100 percent for them, and we want to help them succeed.

WHAT'S STOPPING YOU?

I'm sure you can tell how much I'm committed to the speed of unity . . . and passionate about helping other leaders and their teams get there. I assure you that it will make a profound difference in every aspect of your life and in your organization. This is the future of leadership. The generation that's coming expects to run at the speed of unity.

So, let me ask you: What's stopping you? I believe leaders can find ways to navigate the path to get to the speed of unity, but they're stopped if they don't have two crucial qualities: humility and courage. Some leaders are humble but not courageous. They're gentle and kind, but they don't have the fire to push through the process and make the hard decisions of alignment so they can shift gears. They're humble, but they're afraid of the blowback from the changes. They define unity as the absence of conflict rather than the presence of a common passion, so the most talented and committed people often feel frustrated and leave. But other leaders are courageous but not humble. They have big visions, and they're driven to accomplish a lot, but they haven't developed the empathy necessary to build a cohesive team. They use people instead of leading like a parent—or at least, that's how the people under them feel.

Or do you have that perfect blend of humility and courage? Let's assume you don't! It's very probably an accurate assumption because all of us are a work in progress, no matter what title is on the door of our offices.

WHAT IF . . .?

What if all this happened to you? Wouldn't it be amazing if your team, your company, your church, or your nonprofit was moving at this speed? Don't you want this?

I hope my description of the speed of unity has lit your fire. I hope you're willing to pay the price to shift gears for your team. If you do, it'll bring more joy and meaning to everything you do; it will enrich your life in ways you can't even imagine. Your team will be far more in tune with you than when you moved at the speed of agreement, and you'll get much more accomplished than when you moved at the speed of vision. The impact will outlast you far after you've left the scene because a vibrant, unified culture will be your legacy. And the loving, supportive influence of your team will ripple out into the lives of people beyond your team into your family, your friends, your peers, your customers or members, and to the far reaches of your community.

I HOPE YOU'RE WILLING TO PAY THE PRICE TO SHIFT GEARS FOR YOUR TEAM. IF YOU DO, IT'LL BRING MORE JOY AND MEANING TO EVERYTHING YOU DO; IT WILL ENRICH YOUR LIFE IN WAYS YOU CAN'T EVEN IMAGINE.

My promise is that if you do what it takes to move at the speed of unity, you'll be a better spouse, parent, friend, and leader because your impact will be full of trust, hope, and love. You'll be more secure so you'll be more honest than ever before, you'll be more compassionate because your heart will overflow with kindness, and you'll be more passionate because you won't be afraid to reach for the stars. And you'll be more effective because people will want to follow you.

Don't miss this. It changes everything.

THINK ABOUT IT:

1. Which two or three of the benefits listed in this chapter (personal, family, team, broader audience) is most attractive to you? Explain your answer.

2. How would you define and describe "winning to the third power"?

3. Where are you on the continuum of, on one end, humility without courage . . . and on the other end, courage without humility? What needs to happen so that you develop both so you can lead at the speed of unity?

4. Take a few minutes to daydream about what it will mean to you, your team, and your company, church, or nonprofit to move at top speed.

5. What's your next step?

ENDNOTES

1 Abraham Lincoln, "House Divided Speech," Springfield, Illinois, June 16, 1858, http://www.abrahamlincolnonline.org/lincoln/speeches/house.htm

2 John Foley, "Blue Angels," Executive Forum, http://higher-logicdownload.s3.amazonaws.com/CORENETGLOBAL/f2d6ddf2-66f5-4042-b2ea-71e165781e82/UploadedImages/Articles/Glad+to+be+here+Lessons+in+high+performance+-from+the+Blue+Angels.pdf

3 Jim Collins, "Good to Great," *Fast Company,* September 30, 2001, https://www.fastcompany.com/43811/good-great

4 Phil Jackson, *Eleven Rings: The Soul of Success,* (New York: Penguin Books, 2013), p. 84.

5 Robert Reiss, "How Ritz-Carlton Stays at the Top," Forbes, October 30, 2009, https://www.forbes.com/2009/10/30/simon-cooper-ritz-leader-ship-ceonetwork-hotels.html#39fe2b8c10b1

6 For instance, see "Stress symptoms: Effects on your body and behavior," Mayo Clinic, https://www.mayoclinic.org/healthy-lifestyle/stress-man-agement/in-depth/stress-symptoms/art-20050987 and https://www.mayoclinic.org/healthy-lifestyle/stress-management/in-depth/stress-relief/art-20044464

7 "Protect your brain from stress," *Harvard Health Publishing,* August 2018, https://www.health.harvard.edu/mind-and-mood/protect-your-brain-from-stress

8 Eric Rheam, "Never Look Back! Running Life Lesson #10," https://er-ickrheam.com/2013/06/11/never-look-back-running-life-lesson-10/

9 Recounted in "How This Ex-Con Started from Nothing to Build a 7-Figure Business," Daniel Marlin, *Entrepreneur,* November 16, 2016, https://www.entrepreneur.com/article/284717

10 James M. Kouzes and Barry Z. Pozner, *The Leadership Challenge* (Hoboken, N.J.: Wiley & Sons, 2017), p. 97.

11 Aurel Brudan, "Vision statements as strategic management tools—Historical overview," *Performance Magazine,* July 3, 2010, https://www.performancemagazine.org/vision-statements-as-strategic-management-tools-%E2%80%93-historical-overview/

12 Andy Stanley, *Visioneering* (Colorado Springs: Multnomah Books, 1999), p. 31.

13 Stanley, *Visioneering,* p. 23.

14 Jim Collins, *Good to Great* (New York: HarperCollins, 2001), p. 21.

15 Ibid., p. 22.

16 Eric Baxter, "How NASCAR Drafting Works," Howstuffworks, https://auto.howstuffworks.com/auto-racing/nascar/nascar-basics/nascar-drafting.htm

17 Ed Yong, "Birds That Fly in a V Formation Use an Amazing Trick," *National Geographic,* January 15, 2014, https://www.nationalgeographic.com/science/phenomena/2014/01/15/birds-that-fly-in-a-v-formation-use-an-amazing-trick/

18 Robert Greenleaf, "The Servant as Leader," Greenleaf Center for Servant Leadership, p. 6, https://www.essr.net/~jafundo/mestrado_material_itgjkhnld/IV/Lideran%C3%A7as/The%20Servant%20as%20Leader.pdf

19 Michael Greshko, "The universe seems to be expanding faster than all expectations," *National Geographic,* April 25, 2019, https://www.nationalgeographic.com/science/2019/04/hubble-constant-universe-expanding-faster-than-all-expectations/ (This article will blow your mind . . . if you can understand it!)

20 Hans Tesselaar, "Phil Jackson," *The Los Angeles Times,* June 14, 2011, http://projects.latimes.com/lakers/coach/phil-jackson/

21 For instance, I recommend Dr. Sam Chand's book, *Culture Catalyst.* And if you want more, you can read *The Incestuous Workplace: Stress and Distress in the Organizational Family* by William L. White.

22 Stefano Tasselli, "The Biggest Motivator at Work? Love," *Forbes,* July 16, 2019, https://www.forbes.com/sites/rsmdiscovery/2019/07/16/the-biggest-motivator-at-work-love/#7690620a6d9c

23 Kristen Goodell, "Here's Why Millennials Quit & How to Keep Them," *HRResourceForce,* February 2020, http://www.hrresourceforce.com/why-millennials-quit/

24 Thomas Koulopoulos, "Here's How Great Leaders Listen to and Understand Their Team," *Inc.,* January 6, 2020, https://www.inc.com/thomas-koulopoulos/heres-how-great-leaders-listen-understand-their-team.html

25 "Hearing your own voice," Complete Vocal Institute, https://completevocal.institute/hearing-your-own-voice/

26 Von Ian Kershaw, "How Hitler Won Over the German People," *Spiegel International,* January 3, 2008, https://www.spiegel.de/international/germany/the-fuehrer-myth-how-hitler-won-over-the-german-people-a-531909.html

27 Kenneth Berding, "How Did Early Christians Respond to Plague," Talbot School of Theology, March 16, 2020, https://www.biola.edu/blogs/good-book-blog/2020/how-did-early-christians-respond-to-plagues

28 Lahle Wolfe, "Motives of Passion vs. Money for Starting a Business," the balancecareers, January 21, 2020, https://www.thebalancecareers.com/business-passion-vs-money-3515777

29 Shane Claiborne, *The Irresistible Revolution* (Grand Rapids: Zondervan, 2006), p. 41.

30 Emma Seppälä, "Positive Teams Are More Productive," *Harvard Business Review,* March 18, 2016, https://hbr.org/2015/03/positive-teams-are-more-

31 Lewis Smedes, *Forgive and Forget,* (New York: Harper & Row, 1984), pp. 79-80.

ACKNOWLEDGMENTS

You can't move at the speed of unity with only one person, so I need to say thank you to everyone that has helped me find that speed!

My family, my friends, my mentors, my co-workers and my church family!

We don't always agree on everything, but I thank God we've come together to work through anything. That keeps us from the greatest speed that we've been created for! I'm indebted to you as we race to change the world and grateful for all you mean to me as we race to that end!

ABOUT THE AUTHOR

As Lead Pastor of River Valley Church, Rob Ketterling is highly regarded for his vision and relentless passion to expand the kingdom of God.

He and his wife Becca have been married for over thirty years and launched River Valley in 1995, which has since grown to over 10,000 people with eight locations across the Minneapolis, Minnesota, area and one international campus (Mbekelweni, eSwatini) with plans for further expansion in the future.

Rob has a down-to-earth preaching style, allowing his audience to take practical steps in their journey no matter where they are. He inspires people to live an authentic, faith-filled relationship with Jesus, and he challenges leaders at every level to change the world. He is the author of several books, including *Change Before You Have To, Thrill Sequence, Front-Row Leadership,* and *Fix It!* He currently serves on the Lead Team of the Association of Related Churches (ARC) and the Church Multiplication Network (CMN).

Rob loves traveling and spending time with Becca and his family. Rob and Becca have two sons, Connor and Logan, both on staff at River Valley Church. They're thrilled to welcome Mikayla, Logan's bride, into the family. When Rob isn't at work building the kingdom, he's recharging on the golf course.

DO YOU WANT MORE LEADERSHIP INSIGHT FROM ROB KETTERLING?

We started the River Valley Network for one reason, to help churches succeed and find solutions. We are constantly adding new resources and training opportunities for you and your team. We want to see the local church thrive all over the world and see the kingdom of God move forward! I hope you will be a part of it.

Through a relational and practical coaching style, the River Valley Network exists to help bring solutions for your entire team in the areas of giving, church leadership, worship, the next generation and more!

Leadership insights from
Lead Pastor, Rob Ketterling

Access to key staff leading various
ministry areas of River Valley Church

Invitations to join our ministry-specific groups
focused on community, conversation and
collaboration

Access to Roundtables, one-day Summits,
and special pricing at our annual Conference

Access to a unique collaborative network
of key leaders nationwide

Access to hundreds of unique resources
and creative content including sermon series,
kids curriculum, worship resources, leadership
training, HR documents, and more!

VISIT

NETWORK.RIVERVALLEY.ORG

TO LEARN MORE

RESOURCES

To order more copies of *Speed of Unity* or any of the resources listed on the following pages, go to **resources.rivervalley.org**

FIX IT!

Even before the smoke starts to rise, every leader sees the signals that something isn't right. Your wide variety of problems may vary in severity, scope, and timing, but they have one thing in common: People are looking to you to fix them all!

But before you go running for the fire extinguisher, the duct tape, or to schedule an emergency meeting of your board of elders, see what Pastor Rob Ketterling has to say. It may surprise you to discover that the problem isn't yours to fix.

With wisdom acquired through personal experience and no shortage of trial and error (which he shares with brutal honesty and a large dose of humor), Ketterling will verify that some problems are indeed yours to handle. Other times, however, it's best to delegate the matter to "them" (your staff, lay leaders, volunteers, or whomever), or you risk denying others valuable opportunities to learn and grow. And sometimes, nothing less than a "big boom" from God will resolve a dilemma. The key is to learn which route to take in every situation.

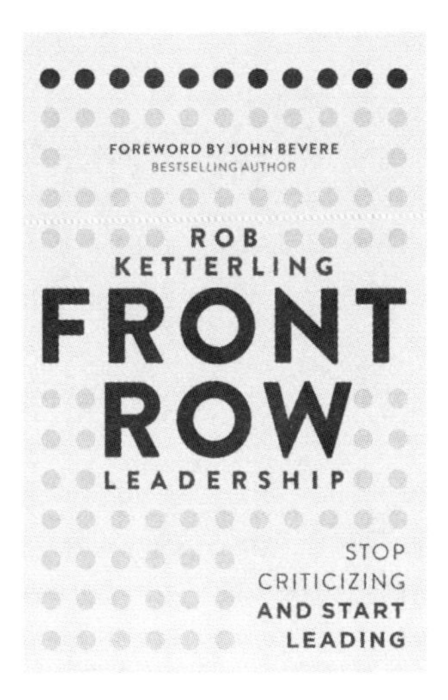

FRONT ROW LEADERSHIP

Become the person of influence you were born to be. Whether you're a CEO, a volunteer, or a homemaker, leadership is your responsibility. Rob Ketterling offers tools that will empower you to move up to the front and lead the change you want to see take place. Learn to engage the leadership process and contribute with your God-given strengths.

THRILL SEQUENCE

Are you constantly looking for your next adrenaline-packed experience? Seeking another dose of excitement from an adventure with suspense, fun, and danger rolled into one? What if your Christian life were just as thrilling? Rob Ketterling encourages readers to seek adventure in a full-on, reignited faith. He challenges others to discover the excitement in passionately pursuing a life of service and reckless faith.

CHANGE BEFORE YOU HAVE TO

What will it take for you to change? For most of us, it takes a crisis, a tragedy, a pain so great that change is actually forced upon us. By then, it's way too late. But what if you could find the strength to change before the pain, before the crisis, before the tragedy? No more excuses, no more good intentions, it's time to change and live life to the fullest!